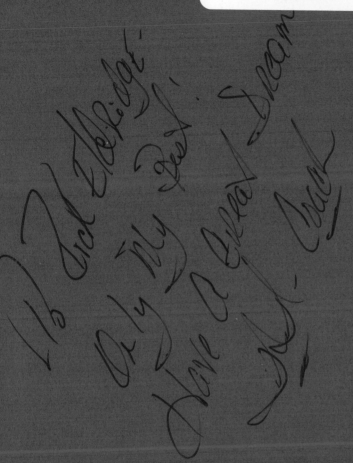

To Rich Eldridge -

Only my Best -

Have A Great Dream

- Coach

TYSON–DOUGLAS

Other Boxing Books from Potomac Books, Inc.

Rocky Lives!: Heavyweight Boxing Upsets of the 1990s,
David Finger

*Boxing's Most Wanted™: The Top 10 Book of Champs,
Chumps, and Punch-Drunk Palookas,*
David L. Hudson Jr., and Michael Fitzgerald Jr.

TYSON–DOUGLAS

THE INSIDE STORY OF
THE UPSET OF THE CENTURY

JOHN JOHNSON
AND
BILL LONG

Potomac Books, Inc.
Washington, D.C.

Library of Congress Cataloging-in-Publication Data
Johnson, John, 1944–
  Tyson-Douglas : the inside story of the upset of the century / John Johnson, Bill Long. — 1st ed.
      p. cm.
  Includes bibliographical references.
  ISBN-13: 978-1-59797-068-6 (alk. paper)
  1. Tyson, Mike, 1966–2. Douglas, Buster, 1960–3. Boxers (Sports)—United States—Biography. 4. Boxing matches—Japan—Tokyo. I. Long, Bill, 1947- II. Title.
  GV1131.J65 2007
  796.83092'2—dc22
  [B]
                          2006037205

Printed in the United States of America on acid-free paper that meets the American National Standards Institute Z39-48 Standard.

Potomac Books, Inc.
22841 Quicksilver Drive
Dulles, Virginia 20166

First Edition

10 9 8 7 6 5 4 3 2 1

To James "Buster" Douglas, Mike Tyson, and all other fighters. I often say I coach the greatest athlete—fighters. *No* athlete pays the price to achieve their dreams as much as a fighter. I salute you, love and respect you for stepping into that ring and putting it all on the line—giving only your best!

To my family: wife Susan, son John II, daughter Mary Catherine, and her husband, Jim, for your love and support. I love you. To my grandchildren: Jordan, Joshua, Bethaney, and Jimmy. May you always pursue your dreams with desire, dedication, and determination. I love you so much. You are the light of my life. Grandaddy.

❐ ❑ ❐

To my dad, Bob Long, my first and best coach.

We never know how high we are
Till we are asked to rise
And then if we are true to plan
Our statures touch the skies—
The Heroism we recite
Would be a daily thing
Did not ourselves the Cubits warp
For fear to be a King
—Emily Dickinson

CONTENTS

ACKNOWLEDGMENTS

No one writes a book alone. Bill Long would like to thank the following people who made this adventure possible:

John Johnson. There would be no book without John. The book was his idea, his dream. We make a great team, John and I; he the ultimate dreamer, me the ultimate cynic. Thank you, John, for choosing me to go along for the ride.

Steve Greenburg, who provided the leadership that helped guide this project from the original idea to the final page.

Nancy Wolske, a friend with an exceptional eye for the written word.

Donna Walls, for her invaluable technical support.

And to my family and friends who put up with me through it all, especially my girl Schmoopie, a man's true best friend.

❏ ❑ ❐

John Johnson would like to thank the following people:

First I want to thank Jesus Christ for his forgiveness. Because of our faith in Him, James and I looked at Mike Tyson as just another man. Not that I believe that Christ takes sides in any athletic contest; I don't. Jesus loves us all the same, no matter what religion, and he wants us to love each other and to care for those in need. Jesus told me to ask people to read Matthew 25:31–46.

I want to thank my family; my wife Susan, my son John, and my daughter Mary Catherine. Your love and support and sacrifice during the six years of my crazy dream for James Douglas to become the heavyweight champion of the world enabled me to achieve that dream.

Coach "Woody" Hayes, you brought out in me what it took to bring out in James Douglas, what most everyone thought was impossible—to defeat the invincible Mike Tyson. Your loyalty, love, and compassion made you a greater man than coach. All those who coached with you, the players who played for you, and all those other people who, fortunately, crossed your path, will never forget you and will always love you.

James Douglas. As I said to you over and over while I hugged your neck after the fight, "James, you were great, you were great!" I want to thank you for the love and friendship that we shared and for the greatness we achieved together. We made our dream come true. You will be remembered in sports history for that one great afternoon in Tokyo.

J. D. McCauley. For having the faith in me to tell James Douglas that he should come to me for help in his career. You were a great part of Buster's success. Together we achieved our goal of James becoming heavyweight champion. And still, today, we have that dream for another fighter. Your loyalty and friendship will remain an important part of my life.

Love him or hate him, I have to thank Don King for giving us the opportunity to fight for the championship. I don't think he ever thought James would defeat Mike Tyson, but nonetheless he gave us that avenue to achieve our dream. He is one of the greatest promoters of all time.

Mike Tyson is a courageous warrior and one of the great heavyweight champions. As I told him in Las Vegas, "I have great respect for you and love for your great effort" in what was one of the most exciting heavyweight battles of all time. Your previous accomplishments created the "Upset of the Century." Thank you.

Thanks to Akihiko Honda for promoting a fight that no one else wanted to promote. It turned out to be the right decision on your part. You promoted boxing's "Upset of the Century" on that one afternoon in Tokyo. And thank you to the Japanese people for their kindness and warmth during our time in their city. They will always be very special people in our lives.

Peyton Sher, your advice throughout the six years helped a

lot. Helping us get the Tex Cobb fight and the fight in your home-town of Duluth, Minnesota, made a big difference in James's career.

Dan Briggs, for giving us space at "Fitness Trend" to put in a gym. I can still see you jumping up and down in the ring in Tokyo. We did it brother!

Ed Ferkany and Dick Walker by helping me get involved with the Ohio State Football Program and Coach Woody Hayes. You helped change my life. You were both great coaches and we have had memorable times together and I shall always appreciate the close friendship we have had.

Pete Johnson, the greatest fullback ever. Because of what we accomplished together, Coach Hayes came to love me and to believe in me, an honor I shall always cherish. Thank you so much, Brother!

Steve Wynn, a brilliant, hard-working man who has achieved greatness in his chosen field of endeavor. Thank you for being a friend during a stressful time in my life. I also thank you and your lovely wife, Elaine, for helping and caring for a lot of people in need, as I have seen you do. You will be the first person I call when I get my next world champion.

Jim Lampley. We first met on the sidelines of an Ohio State–Michigan football game. Little did we know that years later we would be involved in the "Upset of the Century." Thanks so much, Jim, for writing the foreword to this book.

Thanks to Steve Greenburg for sticking with me and giving me great advice in getting *Tyson-Douglas* written and published. You are great at what you do and I will always be grate-ful for your help.

Billy Long, for scoring on that great touchdown run against Purdue to help OSU win the national championship in 1968, and for spending countless hours and putting up with me during the writing of this book. You did great, brother.

Kevin Cuddihy and Potomac Books, Inc., for believing in the story of that one great afternoon in Tokyo. Thank you so much.

FOREWORD

The thing I'll always remember most is the quiet. It was as though we were calling a golf match, or perhaps offering interpretation at an opera, *sotto voce*. Inside the ring the biggest upset in the history of heavyweight championship boxing was taking place. Just off the ring apron, where I sat with Ray Leonard and Larry Merchant, you could hear the gentle slapping of Buster Douglas's and Mike Tyson's shoe soles against the canvas. And if you listened closely, just as if you were alone to monitor sparring in a gym, you could hear that one of the two fighters was leading the dance, surer of his moves, in command of the boxing match.

Some of the quiet could be attributed to shock, as the Tyson-fixated Japanese crowd searched and searched for the cartoon monster they had come to celebrate, and saw only a fighter, on this day a fighter with flaws. Some of the quiet should justifiably be chalked up to awe, the response of media and other ringsiders to the brilliance Douglas was delivering before our disbelieving eyes. And of course it wasn't even dark outside. It was mid-morning Sunday, February 11 in Tokyo, partially an accommodation to an American television audience that was seeing the fight live, in effect the night before, February 10, 1990, the way it appears in ring record books.

In 32 years of network television sports commentary of every kind imaginable, I've never done a stranger or more memorable telecast.

We had covered Tyson in Tokyo before, just less than two years earlier, in a romp over the hapless Tony Tubbs that had been my first telecast as the new blow-by-blow voice of HBO's World Championship Boxing. I had earned a reputation calling several Tyson fights on ABC, his first network exposures, and wound up following the Iron Mike phenomenon to premium cable. Now we were well into the next phase of his career, which had been incubated on the previous trip to Tokyo—married with considerable difficulty to Robin Givens, managed by the actress and her mother, in the promotional clutches of Don King, developing a circus-act life to feed the media monster that both nurtured and mauled him.

If you were paying really close attention, you might have noticed also that his technical skills as a boxer were drifting, that in fights against Frank Bruno and Carl Williams in 1989 he had swung bigger and with fewer combinations. But virtually no one was really looking that closely, nor was much public attention paid to the gradual evaporation of the protective cocoon in which previous managers Jimmy Jacobs and Bill Cayton had protected him. Mike was Mike, Bruno and Williams were easy knockout victims; there was no reason to see Buster Douglas in a different light. The challenge of Tokyo wasn't the fight; it was keeping Mike from going over the edge.

In retrospect a different view does emerge. Tyson was a knockout machine against the 17 carefully chosen victims he blasted to pieces to begin his professional career, 12 of them in the first round. The highlight reel was, indeed, a cartoon. But then he struggled to win a decision against James "Quick" Tillis, his first 10-round fight, and some ringsiders thought a draw would have been more appropriate. Then came another dull decision against Mitch "Blood" Green in Madison Square Garden, before he went into the HBO Heavyweight Championship tournament and beat up shop fighters like Pinklon Thomas and Trevor Berbick. And there were more spectacular knockouts, like Tyrrell Biggs and an ancient Larry Holmes, but there were also 12-round struggles with Tony Tucker and James "Bonehugger" Smith, and a trip to the last 10 seconds or so before he got rid of Jose Ribalta.

What did Tillis, Green, Tucker, Smith, and Ribalta all have in common? They were taller than Mike, and could move around a little (Tillis and Ribalta) or effectively clench Mike inside (Green,

Tucker, and Smith). What kind of fighter was Douglas? A man as tall as any of the others, a far better athlete than all of them, a man who could both move and clench at least as effectively as anyone Mike had fought. Looking back, knowing what we now know about styles, Buster was the prototype for Lennox Lewis—someone who was just too big and too good a boxer for a lunging, one-punch-at-a-time Tyson to ever beat.

But all of that is hindsight. No one, and I mean no one, saw all that before that fateful day in Tokyo. Then, in 10 rounds unfolding like a carefully written stage play, we saw it all, written in the bold strokes of Buster Douglas.

The legitimate, full-blown heavyweight championship of the world is an imposing identity to try on. It requires an irrationally outsized ego to ward off the demons of doubt, the inevitable impostor complex that comes with wearing the largest shoes you can imagine. In the months after he won the crown, Buster Douglas put on enough weight to ensure he'd have a hard time keeping it. The Douglas who beat Mike Tyson on merit in Tokyo would have had significant style advantages against Evander Holyfield in his first defense that fall. But that fighter never showed up in Las Vegas. That fighter vanished the very morning he appeared, on an eerily quiet and unforgettable Sunday morning in Tokyo, author of the greatest heavyweight championship upset in the 115-year history of gloved professional prizefighting. To have been the voice of that event for a live television audience on HBO remains the most distinctive moment from among the five hundred plus championship fights I have called.

Jim Lampley
Los Angeles

INTRODUCTION

The Earth has stopped spinning. Cause and effect has been turned upside down, the laws of physics broken.
                                                      —Max Kellerman, ESPN

Upsets have always been an integral part of sports. Sports wouldn't *be* sports without upsets. I mean, what would college hoops be without North Carolina State's desperate last-second buzzer beater against Hakeem Olajuwon's unbeatable Houston Cougars in the '83 NCAA championship game. (Visions of N. C. State coach Jimmy Valvano racing around the hardwood like a crazy man after the shocking upset are burned into our collective psyche). Or who can forget announcer Al Michaels piercingly counting down those last five seconds in Lake Placid—"Do you believe in miracles?"—as the upstart American hockey team impossibly defeated the indestructible Russian bear in the 1980 winter Olympics. In many ways our sacred world of sports is uniquely defined by the upset. But what really is an upset? In the end, who decides what constitutes an upset in sports? You hear the expression all the time; just listen every day to your sports radio and TV and you'll hear the word *upset* being bantered about in any number of game situations. It's mostly subjective hype. In the end there's only one objective, meaningful place where the term "upset" has any true meaning. Las Vegas. Gambling isn't a game for these sports economists. It's business, big business. They cannot afford to get it wrong in the desert. So, setting a "line" or computing the odds in any sporting event—determining the favorite and the underdog, thus the potential upset—is the main event in Vegas. Put another way, Alan Greenspan wouldn't qualify for a job setting sports lines in Las Vegas. And what is the ultimate goal of the line setter and odds maker? The object is to get as near as the same number of bettors on each side of a bet as is humanly possible. The house doesn't gamble. The house isn't interested in sweating out the outcome of any sports event. Just give them the guaranteed "juice" and the house is happy. That's why the house likes slot machines and that's why the house likes sports betting. There's nothing so rare in life as a sports event in Las Vegas that produces no line or odds. Las Vegas isn't in business to pass on a bet, especially the world heavyweight championship fight. That's exactly what happened in the end with the Tyson-Douglas bout— no odds. Despite the unmatchable skill of Vegas odds makers it was impossible to get anyone to place a bet on Buster Douglas to win the championship against Tyson, no matter the odds. And that makes Buster Douglas the ultimate underdog and his win the ultimate upset in sports history.

 **1**

DOWN GOES TYSON

When Godzilla hit the canvas in the tenth, 30,000 Japanese sat in stunned silence. At ringside, a bleary-eyed Don King and his fading vision of a Tyson-Holyfield match and $20 million, joined them. The cultural freak show that seemed so surreal during the two weeks prior to the greatest upset in sports history had come to a crashing thud. James "Buster" Douglas had just demolished perhaps the scariest fighter of all time. He didn't finesse him. He didn't out-point him. He didn't win in a judges' decision (later it would be learned just how impossible that would've been). Simply put, Douglas kicked Mike Tyson's butt. Gamera defeats Godzilla. This wasn't the script Don King had written. And in the Douglas corner, as a confused and wobbly Tyson fumbled for his mouthpiece and was counted out by referee Octavio Meyran, Douglas's manager, John Johnson, suddenly realized one of his boyhood dreams had just come true.

On February 11, 1990 (February 10 in the United States), in Tokyo, Japan, 1 minute and 23 seconds into the tenth round of a scheduled 12-round heavyweight championship fight, a fight NO ONE predicted would go beyond two rounds, James "Buster" Douglas (29-4-1) knocked out Mike Tyson, the heavyweight champion of the world. Tyson was 37-0 (33 knockouts) and standing on the edge of immortality. He was dismantling opponents at a devastating rate and with such ease the boxing world was beginning to make historic comparisons. Then came Buster Douglas. In hindsight, Tokyo was the beginning of the end for Tyson. As unbeatable a fighter he seemed to be at the time, it now can be said a great part of Mike Tyson's success was the by-product of a terrifying mystique surrounding him. In a sport that thrives on violence and intimidation, Tyson had become the ultimate intimidator. In fact, Tyson had perfected the art. No one really wanted to get into the ring with him. Just weeks before the fight, a major sports magazine claimed that Tyson's unique physical make-up actually made it impossible for him to be knocked out. The boxing experts were starting to believe just that. It could be said that Tyson was beginning to look non-human. A machine designed for the sport, as if a kind of Darwinian evolution had suddenly presented to world the perfect fighter. But in Tokyo Buster Douglas stripped away the mystique and exposed Tyson for what he was, and what he remains to this day.

That's not to take anything away from Douglas, who fought a strategic, gutsy fight. He was as focused and determined as any fighter who ever stepped into the ring. Except for one punch in the eighth round, Douglas controlled the entire fight, totally frustrating Tyson. And Mike Tyson still was an extremely intimidating figure. He didn't knock out 33 opponents—his five previous heavyweight title fights averaged less than three rounds—by simply stepping into the ring.

LOYALTY

Buster Douglas was, well, "top of the world, ma." You might say it was Lula Pearl Douglas who knocked out Mike Tyson on that strange afternoon in Tokyo, Japan. Lula Pearl was Buster's beloved mother who passed away three weeks before the biggest day of her boy's life. In fact, just minutes after the historic knockout, Buster dedicated the championship to her. "God bless her heart."

History shows Douglas's fighting career (and life) was marked during those 10 rounds in Tokyo. At no time before or since would the world of Buster Douglas come into such sharp focus. Some people's lives turn out that way. Special people. Most never have a single second that compares to that moment when Douglas saw Tyson fumbling on the canvas in the tenth round trying instinctively to put his mouthpiece back in its place; that's precisely when Douglas realized Tyson was finished, and he knew he was the heavyweight champion of the world. The experts are still shaking their heads, trying to explain how the impossible happened. It was literally the fight of a lifetime.

So how does a story such as this unfold? How can a person who was described by *Columbus Dispatch* sports writer Tim May as, "a man like flowing water, he will always take the path of least resistance," become the fighter portrayed by John Ed Bradley of *Sports Illustrated* after the Tyson fight: "What Buster Douglas did in the ring was heroic, he *was* Rocky." Did the force of gods and nature come together at just the right moment in time, pointing a fateful finger at Douglas, saying it was his time? Is that how these historic moments happen?

James "Buster" Douglas was born on April 7, 1960, in Columbus, Ohio. Boxing flowed in Douglas's veins. In fact, Douglas took to boxing as far back as he can remember, "just to get close to my dad." Buster's dad, Bill "Dynamite" Douglas, was becoming a boxing legend in Columbus while Buster was growing up. When the elder Douglas was in the ring, he was on a killing mission. He was one of the toughest fighters who ever stepped into a boxing ring that you've never heard of. As for Buster's mom, Lula Pearl, well, the son admits today that his mother's full-time job was pampering her boy. "She would let me do what I pleased, when I was pleased to do it." But in the end, it was dad who Buster had to go to for resolution. For years, Douglas's dad kept his son out of the gym. But at age 10, Douglas finally convinced his father to let him see the inside of the fighting world. Young Douglas was like most sons; he wanted to be his dad. He wanted to be the warrior he saw in his father. However, the two couldn't have been more dissimilar. The story is told that the elder Douglas once went 10 grueling rounds in a fight, taking his opponent apart, only to retire to the locker room afterwards to shadow box another three rounds against a ghost opponent. Young Douglas stood in the shadows of the locker room that night watching this driven, giant man rage against whatever demons he had to conquer. But he would never have his dad's drive, or the ferocity that might have changed the legacy of his boxing career.

Still, he had potential and once his dad saw it the father took up the charge of training his boy. Buster was thrilled, a son's dream fulfilled. For the next several years they worked as a team, traveling around the state of Ohio, fighting amateur matches, honing the young boy's fighting skills. This was the best of times for Buster, and he got to know his father as he never had before. Although the result of this father-and-son boxing team was a Golden Gloves championship for Buster at age 15, the relationship was already wearing thin. Buster just didn't have his father's heart and drive, or his killer instinct. This lack of passion drove Bill Douglas crazy and, eventually, away from his son. His father's intensity was also too much for Buster, and Buster turned to normal high school activities, with a state basketball championship resulting. But in 1981, finally realizing that his great natural abilities were in the ring, Buster decided boxing was the only way to the top of the sports world. So, father and son teamed up again for the beginning of Buster's professional career. It was an uneasy alliance, and a string of nondescript fights followed. Buster was sleepwalking through his boxing career. This is not a sport to pursue half-heartedly. He didn't have focus, he wouldn't train, and he lacked the craving of a champion. Only Buster's great natural abilities kept him from getting injured in the ring. His father would walk away again, but Bill Douglas couldn't stay away from his son for good, he would eventually find his way back to Buster's corner.

Like many sons, Buster had issues with his father. As Johnson puts it, "In the ring, Bill Douglas was a violent man." It's a description that would *never* follow the son. Bill "Dynamite" Douglas still is a boxing legend in Columbus, Ohio; Buster Douglas was only the heavyweight champion of the world.

Bill Douglas would walk away from his son, and his son would call on John Johnson. Their first meeting was the beginning of an historic journey, the first step to the world championship.

❐ ❑ ❐

To Douglas's manager John Johnson, the most important trait in a man is loyalty. You sense it the moment you meet the lanky, easy-going West Virginian with the uncommon, yet inviting drawl. Johnson never goes anywhere without his three Michigan gold-pants medals hanging from a gold chain around his neck (Ohio State football players and coaches are given a solid gold-pants medal for defeating arch-rival Michigan), his huge world championship ring (designed by Buckeye All-American and Outland/Lombardi winner Jim Stillwagon), a Big Ten championship ring (Johnson has three), and the scarlet and grey leather Ohio State jacket. Johnson is a steadfast Buckeye who'll tell you his mentor, the legendary Woody Hayes, taught him loyalty. Johnson met Hayes in the spring of 1972, and that meeting changed his life. Not until that tenth round in Tokyo would anything else ever come close in significance.

Johnson believes any dream is possible. "You just have to make it happen," he always says. When you consider John Johnson's life, it makes perfect sense. He's lived the American dream. Born in Red Jacket, West Virginia, "just a few miles from the end of the road," Johnson had two dreams while growing up in those tree-covered hills. He wanted to play football for the Ohio State Buckeyes and he wanted to be heavyweight champion of the world. A pretty tall order for a skinny country kid who learned early on from his mom that rock throwing was the best defense against the bullies from over the next hill.

Johnson had followed the Columbus boxing scene ever since he arrived in the capital city. He knew Buster and he knew Buster's dad. More importantly, from the first moment he saw Buster work in the ring he knew there was a champion lurking within. The young man would just need a guiding force to drive it home. Johnson would be that force, the coach he'd always believed he could be since the day Woody Hayes stood by him in that small office in the north facility on Ohio State University's campus and changed his life forever. A confidence had surged over him that day. Woody's force had grabbed Johnson and never would let go. Now, as Johnson watched Buster work in the ring he could see the future unfolding before him, like a motion picture. He just had to get Buster to see the greatness trapped inside. It was 1984 but Johnson remembers the beginning of the relationship as if it were yesterday. "I brought out an empty paper plate and laid it on the floor and told James, 'This is what we have, but if you will pay a great price and get in great shape, you'll be the heavyweight champion of the world and there will be millions on this plate.'" Buster made the commitment with Johnson that day, and six years later they were in the corner together facing Godzilla.

 **3**

THE COACH

No sons a bitch fires my coaches but me!
—Woody Hayes

It wasn't always the dream life for John Johnson. The trip from the "end of the road" in Red Jacket to Tokyo was a winding one. Moving from West Virginia to Ohio, he graduated from Bucyrus High School in 1962. After high school Johnson attended the Marion branch of The Ohio State University for one quarter. In November of that year Johnson proposed to his high school sweetheart, Susan Kay Shingledecker (they have been married for 43 years), and began walking the streets of Columbus looking for work. A company, Community Finance, and a hiring manager from Kentucky appeared just in time to put food on the table. Johnson swears to this day he was hired only because in desperation he had pleaded that southerners should stick together. "No other reason to hire me," he says. It was January 13, 1964, and in less than a year Johnson became the youngest manager in the history of the consumer finance industry. He would stay in the finance business for seven years. He was a district manager when a chance meeting on a downtown Columbus street corner caused his true destiny to unfold.

Dick Walker was a local legend in Columbus. A successful high school football coach, he was hired directly from Bishop Watterson High School to coach defensive backs for Hayes. His coaching abilities never were in question, but where Walker really excelled was in the competitive world of college recruiting. He knew how to relate to the young kids. So did Johnson, and the two hit it off immediately. Dick Walker introduced Johnson to Ed Ferkany, also an assistant coach at OSU. John helped both Walker and Ferkany recruit and they both recommended him to Coach Hayes. By the end, Dick Walker would say, "If Woody Hayes had five people he trusted most put on one hand, John Johnson would be on his hand."

Recruiting is mostly out of town, night work, and Walker and Johnson were born for the job. Hayes wanted the boys signed, and Walker and Johnson obliged. But eventually Johnson wanted more. He wanted to get closer to Hayes, and he was beginning to believe he could actually coach; Walker and Ferkany encouraged him in this belief and put in a good word for him with Hayes. So early one morning in the spring of 1972, in the north facility (Woody wanted to call the OSU practice facility Stalag Hayes), John got up the nerve to confront "The Man." Johnson tells it like this: "Coach, I'm not really happy in the finance business and I want to be a football coach."

He got Woody's attention, "John, come and help me coach," Hayes responded, putting his huge arm around him. So from 1973 to 1976 the country kid from Red Jacket, West Virginia, was a graduate assistant football coach at The Ohio State University. Not *exactly* his first boyhood dream, but damn close. During those years, Johnson would earn his bachelor's degree, his master's degree, and all hours toward a doctorate. He also moonlighted at the Anheuser-Busch brewery to supplement his meager coaching salary. The night job would lead to Johnson's most memorable moment with Coach Hayes.

There's an old story floating around Columbus that when Hayes was first hired, he overheard a neighbor speculating on how quickly this new coach would be terminated, just like his predecessors. (Ohio State was considered the graveyard of coaches when Woody took the job) So Hayes immediately set his watch back one hour. Hayes's credo was: "You work harder and longer than your enemy." Johnson didn't need to hear the old story because he observed first hand Hayes's early morning work routine. Johnson quickly seized the moment and began showing up in the football office at 5:30 A.M. to help Woody break down game film. It was then that their relationship was forged. Johnson understood the legendary football coach, and he has his three gold–pants medals and three Big Ten championship rings to prove it.

Another lightning bolt would strike, moving Johnson along on his incredible journey. Part of Johnson's duties for Hayes included working with the scout team. This squad was made up of freshman, walk-ons, old veterans who never made it, and anyone else the coaches could dredge up. Their job is simple: emulate the opposing team each day in practice and generally get mauled by the starting offense and defense while doing it. Insiders at Ohio State call them the AYOs, the acronym for All You Others. Johnson took this job seriously, as he did all his work for the coach. It was here he saw an All American in the making, Pete Johnson. Pete was a big, raw, diamond-in-the-rough freshman fullback from Fort Valley, Georgia, and Long Beach, New York. Johnson liked Pete the first moment he watched the big kid run over, through, and around OSU's starting defense. Most freshmen at this level fall prey to veterans who pressure new recruits to ease off in practice. "Take it easy now kid; your time will come later," they would say. Pete didn't give a damn for them. He kicked ass every play and every day. And this young man could kick some serious ass. As an 18 year old, Pete weighed 245 pounds and could run at you all day long. But Pete failed to make the traveling squad. Pete was feeling abandoned and he told Johnson he was going to leave and go to another school. Johnson went to Coach Hayes and told him Pete was thinking of leaving.

The next week Pete made the traveling team. OSU was playing Iowa and in the second half Pete got in and scored two touchdowns. He then scored the winning touchdown against Michigan. In the Rose Bowl against Southern California that same year, Pete scored three touchdowns; now the entire nation knew the name Pete Johnson. But the Pete Johnson saga wasn't nearly concluded.

One day in January after the first quarter of school, Hayes called Johnson at home and told him to get his ass into the office. Johnson had no idea what he had done wrong, but hustled over to find out. Hayes met him on the way to the meeting and told him immediately, "You can do it John, you can and will." Puzzled, Johnson asked, "do *what*, coach?" Hayes's response: "Help Pete get through school. He could be the greatest fullback ever, but he's not so great in school." Johnson promised Hayes that he'd take the player under his wing and make sure he concentrated on his schoolwork. "I'll never forget my time at Ohio State working with Coach Johnson," says Pete Johnson, reflecting back on his college football career. "We were like brothers."

Pete was a very intelligent young man but had not applied himself in the classroom, due to his being down over not getting to play. Once he started to work hard on his classes, he became the first black Academic All-American football player in Ohio State history.

It was during this period when Hayes taught Johnson the law of loyalty. The OSU athletic director at the time was Ed Weaver. The athletic director's office oversees sports academics at the university, which was the reason Johnson met Weaver. It wasn't a friendly relationship; Weaver just didn't like Johnson's style. Very soon after Pete rehabilitated his grades, Johnson was called into Weaver's office. Weaver accused John of illegally providing football tickets to his teamster friends from Anheuser-Busch and fired Johnson on the spot. Johnson told Weaver he didn't do anything illegal, that his friends had purchased the tickets within university guidelines. It made no matter to the athletic director. He said he didn't like Johnson's attitude and fired him for that.

Johnson sought out Hayes. He found him at the north facility in his closet of an office. (It literally *is* a closet now.) Eyes downcast, Johnson summoned up his courage, told Hayes what had transpired, and closed with, "Coach, Ed Weaver said to tell you I was fired. He didn't like my attitude."

"He can't fire you, you work for me," Woody responded, his face already turning red.

Furious, Hayes called his boss and let him have it. The conversation went something like this: "Ed, no sons a bitch fires my coaches but me. This man's done more for my football program in one year than you have in your entire goddamn career." Click.

At that moment Johnson would've walked through the gates of hell for his boss. He still would.

"Now you get back to work, John."

Johnson would stay on as an assistant coach at OSU through the 1975 season. It was a great season for the Buckeyes but a loss to UCLA in the Rose Bowl kept Woody from another National Championship. Johnson is convinced if the Buckeyes would've ended the '75 season as national champions Woody would have retired immediately and his career-ending disgrace would not have been part of the great coach's legacy.

4

THE MEETING

*Buster Douglas won every fight that Don King wanted him
to lose and lost every fight that Don King wanted him to win.*
—J. D. McCauley

The year was 1984, and John Johnson was at Veteran's
Memorial in downtown Columbus, Ohio, watching a local boxing exhibition. Two white heavyweights—Kip Kane, now a local
high school football coach, and Jeff Jordan—were fighting in the
main event. They'd drawn a big crowd, and Johnson recalls
having to leave the fight early to attend a church function with
his wife, Sue. As he was leaving the building Johnson saw Buster
and his uncle, Sherman Daniels, standing in the lobby. As he
walked toward them to say hello Johnson remembers thinking
that the crowd inside the hall was watching the wrong fighters. No disrespect to Kane or Jordan—both were tough kids and
outstanding fighters—but neither possessed anything close to the
talent, power, and potential of Buster Douglas, and Johnson
knew it. Johnson shook hands with Buster and his uncle that
night, telling Buster he'd seen him fight as a kid and thought
he had great potential. He handed Buster his card and told him
to call if he could help. The card read, "Have a great dream—
Coach J."

A few weeks later Johnson got the call. At the time he was
working for the Ohio Department of Youth Services in charge of
recreational activities for kids incarcerated for criminal activity,
a job Johnson still talks about as his most rewarding work outside
the time spent in the ring with his fighters. He had just returned

from lunch and there was a message waiting for him on his desk. The message read, "please return a call to James Duglas." (Johnson framed the misspelled message.) The date was April 7, 1984, which just happens to be Buster's birth date. Johnson called Buster immediately, addressing him on the phone as James, which he always does when speaking to him directly. "Buster" was a nickname bestowed on him as an infant by J. D. McCauley, Sr., James's grandfather, and the name just stuck through the years.

As it turned out, it was Buster's uncle, J. D. who had suggested that Buster call Johnson and sign him on as his manager. J. D. had reminded Buster what Johnson did for Steve Gregory's boxing career and thought the two should get together and talk. Steve Gregory was Johnson's first fighter. In December 1979, Johnson, along with his partner, the legendary Angelo Dundee, had taken Gregory to the world championship in Copenhagen, Denmark, against Ayub Kalule. Johnson will tell you today that most of what he's learned about the world of boxing came from the precious time with Dundee. J. D. told Buster that he thought Johnson could get him to the heavyweight world title, and Buster believed him.

The meeting was set up for a week later at Johnson's house. Johnson wanted some time to make phone calls and see what the boxing community was saying about the Columbus boxer. By then, Douglas had been fighting for several years (his record was an uninspiring 18-3-1) but he'd taken some time off. He was now thinking of restarting his boxing career, which is what initiated the talk between Douglas and his uncle, which, in turn, led to calling Johnson. So Johnson started making calls, and what he learned wasn't exactly what he was hoping for. As Johnson clearly recalls there just wasn't a lot of excitement out there. The boxing world wasn't saying, "Great, bring on your man and let's do some business." The response was lukewarm at best, and Johnson realized that getting this kid back on track and headed toward a title bout wasn't going to be easy. For that reason, on the night of the meeting with Buster, Johnson invited his good friend Oren Holman to join the group. Holman was his insurance man and Johnson had known him for a long time. Johnson knew that he didn't have the money to back Douglas and that he might have to borrow from Holman to get things started. He wanted Holman to meet Douglas—that was the first step. He'd already told his friend that he thought Douglas could go all the way but he wanted him to size Douglas up himself. It was that night, after they'd all been talking, that Johnson went to the kitchen and brought back the empty plate.

The team all agreed, right there in Johnson's living room, what everyone's commitment would be. Buster Douglas committed to working hard and doing whatever it took to reach the team's goal—that being, of course, the world heavyweight title. Johnson became Douglas's manager, and Oren Holmen put up a couple thousand dollars to take financial pressure off Buster and clear up a few debts. J. D. McCauley would be handling Buster's daily training schedule; it was time to improve Buster's work ethic if they were serious about the team's mission.

Johnson again began making phone calls, finally setting their first fight for July 9, 1984, against a big, rangy white kid from Cincinnati, Ohio, named Dave Starkey. Johnson was confident that Buster could take Starkey but he was a little worried about the opponent's reach. Starkey was 6-8 and Buster had never fought anyone that size before.

Also at that point, Team Douglas was about to get a new member. Bill Douglas was very proud and supportive of his son. He'd managed Buster's career for the previous 22 fights while desperately trying to draw out a more passionate side of his young son. John Johnson had followed Bill Douglas's boxing career years before and they had become friends before Johnson became involved with Buster's career. Johnson fondly recalls a night in West Virginia with Bill, years before Johnson became involved with Buster. The two boxing buddies were in a local club when Bill suddenly got off his bar stool and began to sing a song in front of the entire crowded bar. Johnson was shocked at the sight of the elder Douglas grabbing the mic and busting into song. But Bill Douglas had a voice and he loved to perform; he received a standing

ovation that night in Johnson's home state. After Johnson became Buster's manager, however, the longtime friendship with
the father was destined to fail. Bill Douglas quickly grew to re-
sent Johnson's management role and influence on Buster. And
Bill wasn't going to go away without a fight. So right before
Buster's first match for Johnson, Bill Douglas inserted himself
into the new Buster Douglas–John Johnson team.

John Johnson would, however, find himself thinking about
what it would have been like to work with a fighter with the com-
bined talent and nature of Bill and Buster Douglas. Johnson is
convinced the dream combination would result in perhaps the
greatest fighter of all time. He still believes Bill Douglas could
have been the middleweight champion of the world. The problem was that nobody really wanted to fight Bill Douglas because
of his tenacious nature and his size. In fact, Bill and his manager,
Ralph "Red" Banks, actually invented a new boxing division because Bill just couldn't consistently keep his weight at the 160-
pound division, and he was too small to make the light
heavyweight division. So Red created the 168-pound *super*
middleweight division for his fighter and eventually organized a
title match at the "new" division. Everyone in the boxing world
thought it was a joke at first, but the division lives to this day.

But back to Buster's fight with Starkey. In the first round
Buster hit Starkey with a hard right hand and Starkey started to
go down, his right knee barely touching the canvas. It became a
little confusing at that point and he may have been trying to get
back up, but Buster followed with a left hook. Starkey went down
again, but then, to the crowd's great surprise, he got up, ran across
the ring and tried to pick Buster up and body-slam him to the
canvas. From that point on the whole thing was completely out of
control and, eventually, everybody was in the ring trying to break
up the melee. Both fighters were disqualified. Later, in the dressing room, a very heated exchange between Bill Douglas and J. D.
McCauley ended with Bill leaving Buster again.

After that fight Johnson was desperate to get Buster another
match. It did not come together quickly. Finally, a man out of Kansas

City, Missouri, named Peyton Sher who had worked all of Don King's behind-the-scenes operations for a long time, came through. Johnson had been hounding Sher about Buster for months. As Johnson always says, "You got to wear down their resistance with your persistence." It was early November 1984, and Douglas was now training at the Thompson Center in Columbus, Ohio. Sher told Johnson that a boxer named Randall "Tex" Cobb was supposed to be fighting Trevor Berbick later in the month, but no one was sure that Berbick was going to show for the fight. Sher wanted to know if Douglas would agree to take the fight if necessary. He'd have to go to Vegas—the fight was set up in the Riviera Hotel back parking lot—and if Berbick didn't step on the scales for the weigh-in Buster would simply replace him right there for the fight against Cobb. J. D. and Johnson wanted to do it but Buster needed to be convinced, and Johnson really didn't know why. He would push Buster hard for this fight, telling Buster he was more talented than Cobb and would have no problem kicking his ass—the usual prefight pep talk. But what Johnson was really thinking about was getting their chance with King. He knew the fight wasn't a guaranteed win for Douglas—Cobb is one of the toughest fighters who ever lived and Johnson had tremendous respect for him—but he desperately understood that the road to the world title would eventually go through Don King.

Finally, worn down by his uncle and Johnson, Buster agreed. Buster and J. D. flew out to Vegas early, but Johnson couldn't take the time off from work to go with them. When he finally arrived in Vegas, Johnson recalls that it was right before the prefight press conference and J. D. grabbed him immediately saying, "Oh, man, am I happy to see you. All Buster's been saying is when's Johnny gonna get here, when's Johnny gonna get here?" That was the first time, Johnson says, that he knew their working relationship was finally coming together. Johnson also recalls that when King introduced him during the prefight press conference, King elaborated on Johnson's past involvement and relationship with Woody Hayes and the Ohio State football program. Before that press conference Johnson never realized what an Ohio State/

Woody Hayes fan Don King was. As Johnson puts it, you just can't calculate the influence Woody Hayes had on people. It's here that Johnson relates his favorite Woody story, which involves Richard Nixon.

Johnson, Hayes, and some of the other Ohio State coaches were meeting and the subject of Nixon resigning came up. Hayes, an admirer of the president, was adamant that he should not. After others opined that Nixon might do just that, Hayes demanded a telephone, called the White House, and per the standard at the time gave his phone number to be called back. Upon receiving the call, Hayes stated, "This is Coach Woody Hayes at Ohio State University, let me talk to the president." Bold, but it worked, as the next words out of his mouth were "Mr. President, this is Woody Hayes." Hayes proceeded to inform Nixon that he should not resign, and for the next 30 minutes gave the president his opinion on any number of topics in a non-stop soliloquy that went barely interrupted by Nixon. "I'm sure Nixon on the other end was saying, 'Yep, you're right, Woody," joked Johnson.

Some time later Don King was headed for Columbus with Larry Holmes to attend the annual Touchdown Club Banquet. Before the banquet King called Johnson saying he'd be forever in his debt if Johnson would arrange for an introduction and photo-op with Woody. So Johnson went to Woody and said, "Coach, I need a favor."

"What favor is that, John?" Woody asked.

"Well," Johnson hesitated before he continued. "I need you to meet Don King and have a picture taken with him."

Woody said, "I'm not getting my picture taken with Don King and that's that!" Eventually Johnson prevailed and the picture was taken at the banquet.

Throughout his time with Buster, Johnson had a good working relationship with Don King and always thought highly of him. Johnson describes King as an extremely hard working and brilliant guy who has influenced boxing as much as anyone else in the history of the sport. Johnson's problems with King didn't begin until after the fight in Tokyo, and he thinks to this day of how different it all could have been. The day before the fight Johnson had bragged to anyone who'd listen that Buster was going to kick Tyson's ass. King came to Johnson and said that if Buster won the fight, King would accompany everyone back to Columbus for a big celebration. Well, Buster did kick Tyson's ass and King didn't come back to Columbus to celebrate, the beginning of the end for team Johnson and King.

Back to Las Vegas and the parking lot of the Riviera hotel. Berbick didn't show that night and Buster stepped onto the scales for the fight. It was November 9, 1984, and the fight was what those in the business call a "walk-out" match. That's the fight *after* a championship bout that takes place while everyone is walking out of the arena. Johnson says the parking lot was virtually empty that night and he'll never forget what happened. For the first four rounds Tex Cobb bullied Buster all over the ring, pounding Buster's face and chest. At the end of the fourth, Johnson lost it. Frustrated and angry he got in Buster's face in the corner and started yelling, telling him that they hadn't come all the way to Vegas to lose the fight. Johnson didn't want to see his fighter's restarted career ending abruptly in the back lot of a Vegas hotel. Something must have sunk in because Buster went out the last six rounds and knocked Cobb around like a ping-pong ball, winning the fight in a majority decision. Later, Buddy LaRosa, Aaron Pryor's manager, told Johnson that it was some of the best corner work he'd ever seen in his life.

Johnson and the Douglas team were staying next door to the Riviera at a place called the El Camino. The morning after the fight Johnson and Douglas were sitting in the El Camino lobby when Tex Cobb got off the elevator. Striding across the lobby to shake Buster's hand, Cobb smiled and said, "Great job, big boy. Maybe we can do it again sometime." Johnson and Douglas looked at each other as Cobb walked away, both thinking the same thing; you don't go to war with someone like Tex Cobb unless you have to. Buster didn't want to get in the ring again with Tex Cobb.

The next fight followed a call from Bruce Trampler, a matchmaker for Top Rank, who was sponsoring a heavyweight tournament in Atlantic City, and wanted to know if Buster wanted in. Johnson immediately said yes. Four heavyweight fighters would compete in this tournament on March 27, 1985; Buster would be fighting Dion Simpson. Johnson was worried; Buster was not in great shape, nowhere near where he needed to be to compete for the world title. In fact, he weighed in that night at around 240 pounds. As it turned out, though, there was no need for concern; Buster knocked out Simpson in the first round with an overhand right.

The team moved on to another fight in Atlantic City on May 9, 1985, against Jesse Ferguson. This would be the final fight of the Top Rank tournament, and again, Buster wasn't in great shape. He lost to Ferguson that night in a majority decision after 10 rounds. In an all-too-often theme at this point in Douglas's career, he lost because he wasn't in top fighting condition. Johnson believes it's fair to say that Buster's biggest, most critical flaw was his lack of intensity in training. It was, in part, what drove his dad away from him. Because of this major flaw, Johnson's most difficult challenge in managing Douglas was motivating him. In all of his years in the boxing business Johnson never saw another boxer with anything close to Buster's talent. (That is, of course, with the exception of Muhammad Ali.)

On the way home from Atlantic City that night, J. D. asked Buster if he thought he might have done better if his dad had been in the corner with him. Buster said yes.

The Douglas team went from May 1985 to January 1986 without a fight. The next break came when, again, Peyton Sher called with an offer, and it was a big one. This would be a fight against Greg Page in Atlanta, Georgia, on the undercard of the Tim Witherspoon and Tony Tubbs heavyweight championship fight. On this night, Jan. 17, 1986, Buster's dad would be back in the corner. Also on this night, the boxing world would see Buster Douglas in the best shape he'd ever been since his partnership with Johnson began. Everyone was psyched—Buster wanted the fight and it would show in the ring later that night. It was, Johnson says, the best fight of Buster's career up to that point.

Now, Greg Page put up a gallant fight that night too, and Johnson believes that if he'd trained harder and avoided certain out-of-the-ring problems he could have been a world champion again also. Both fighters landed outstanding jabs and vicious punches, and there were some heated exchanges before the fight ended. Johnson thought that Buster was winning, but he also knew it would be one of those decisions that could go either way. They ended up, however, with a unanimous decision, and Johnson was so pumped he called Peyton Sher right after the fight. Nobody had really given Buster a chance to win the fight. He was a major underdog, not as much so as in the Tyson fight, but still a major underdog. Johnson gave Sher a percentage of his take on the fights he'd set up for Buster, but he was so broke on the night of that phone call that he asked Sher to reduce his percentage in exchange for five percent of Buster's entire contract. Sher wouldn't do it and, of course, as things turned out, Johnson would be damned grateful he didn't.

It was after this fight that Johnson signed a promotional agreement with Don King and was, finally, on the right path. Now it was back to the Las Vegas Hilton for the next fight. This time it was April 19, 1986, and it was the undercard again. Buster's opponent was, in Johnson's words, a tough-assed kid from Toledo named Dave Jaco. Jaco had a brother who played football for the Buckeyes. Jaco was bright, not a great technical boxer, and real tough. The fight went the distance—8 rounds—and Douglas won in a decision, but the fight was a setback for him. Johnson felt, with all due respect to their opponent, the fight shouldn't have gone past the first round. Jaco wasn't in the same league as Douglas, and the only reason the fight went 8 rounds was that Buster, once again, wasn't in fighting shape. Buster's dad and J. D. went at each other again in the corner during the fight, and team Douglas went from the total elation they had all felt after the Page fight to public bickering, and a fighter was headed in the wrong direction.

September 6, 1986, would be the next fight, this time against Dee Collier. Buster won the fight in a decision, but Johnson was again disappointed—he knew it wasn't a great showing. They went then from September '86 to May 30, 1987, without a fight—a long and very stressful eight months for the team. Relations between J. D. McCauley and Bill Douglas were getting worse by the day and Johnson was exhausted from trying to play referee and pestering Don King for more fights.

Finally, the big call came. King was ready to give them their first shot at a title, setting up a special tournament with Buster fighting Tony Tucker for the International Boxing Federation (IBF) world championship. Mike Tyson would be fighting "Bonecrusher" Smith, with the winners meeting for a combination championship.

Prior to the Tucker fight Johnson went to a friend, Danny Briggs, who owned a gym in Columbus called Fitness Trend. Danny was a former Columbus Clippers baseball player. Johnson told him that Buster would be fighting for the world championship and needed a permanent training facility. Briggs gave them a small space near the basketball and aerobic areas, where Johnson had Red Banks (Bill Douglas's former manager) and his brother Bob build a full-scale boxing ring. This was the first time Buster Douglas had a permanent training facility.

Johnson and the team decided to bring in a special sparring partner for Buster to get him ready for the fight. Aaron Snowell, Tyson's future trainer, brought them a young, hard-hitting kid named Mike Evans. At some point during the training he badly bruised Douglas's ribs, prompting Johnson to go to the Ohio State football trainers for a special rib guard used to protect quarterbacks. Bill Douglas was again working with J. D. and the training was especially rough. Buster showed unusual willingness to do the work for this fight, but the tensions outside the ring were worse than ever. Everyone knew it, but no one could stop it. J. D. and Buster's dad were openly at each other.

A second special sparring partner was brought in after Mike Evans was sent home, a young man by the name of Darnell Hayes, who was actually a light heavyweight. This paid off as Hayes proved to be invaluable in improving Buster's quickness. In fact, he ended up going out to Vegas with the team for the actual fight and was in the corner with Buster's dad and Eddie Aliano, one of the great cut men of all time. J. D. and Johnson, however, were noticeably absent from the corner that night—Bill Douglas was doing his best to ease them out of the inner circle.

During the actual fight, J. D. and Johnson sat together at ringside. Johnson would relate later that it was one of the hardest things he would ever have to do. The fight was very close from the beginning, but Johnson and J. D. felt that Buster was slightly ahead in points. Then, all of a sudden, in the tenth round, Tucker managed to back Buster into the ropes and began hitting him with some good shots. Buster didn't respond. The referee stopped the fight and, just like that, the fight was over. The locker room was a sad and angry place that night.

The next morning Johnson brought Buster's check to him in his hotel suite. He remembers that he wanted Buster to speak first. He wanted to know what Buster was thinking because he knew there would never be a more critical time in their working relationship, or in Buster's career. When he did finally speak, Buster was near tears as he said, "Dad has to go. I can't take any more of this dissension—he has to go."

Johnson is careful to stress here the importance of what Buster said that morning. Contrary to what most people believe, it was never Johnson's decision to drop Bill Douglas—it was Buster's and Buster's alone. After Buster told him this Johnson asked him what his intentions were. Buster, without hesitation, replied that it was his intention to follow their common dream. From that point until Tokyo, Johnson was involved in every aspect of Buster's career, including the daily training. For the first time Johnson insisted on beginning an extensive weight-training and running program, and Johnson and J. D. also stepped up their fighter's gym work. The new regime wasn't easy but Buster knew it had to be done.

There was, however, a new wrench in the works. Don King stopped talking to them. King was extremely upset over Buster's performance in the Tucker fight, believing that Buster simply quit in the tenth and that both Buster and Johnson let King down. At least that's what King was saying to the public at this time. In his mind, King had given Douglas and his team a shot at the title and they blew it—simple as that. So the team went from May to November 1987 without a fight.

Desperate to jump-start Buster's flagging career, Johnson again borrowed money from his old friend, Oren Holman, to put together a boxing event in Buster's hometown, Columbus, Ohio. They were training hard and J. D. was doing an outstanding job of keeping Buster motivated both in and out of the gym. J. D. woke Buster every day at 5:30 A.M. to run in Sharon Woods, and train at the gym. Johnson recalls himself acting like his old mentor, Woody Hayes, in his effort to keep Buster focused. Lots of chairs were thrown in that gym during those months by Buster, but they needed a fight and were willing to do whatever it took to get one.

At his own event, Johnson paired Buster against a young fighter from Youngstown, Ohio, named Donny Long. It was November 19, 1987, and proved to be not much of a fight, as Buster stopped his opponent in the second round. Johnson did get a little scared in that fight, though; Buster had landed a somewhat "late" punch that ended the fight, and Johnson worried that the boxing commission might suspend Buster like they did before. Fortunately, they didn't.

A few months later Peyton Sher again stepped in, setting up a fight for February 24, 1988, in Duluth, Minnesota. This would be against Purcell Davis, a veteran fighter. Buster still wasn't in the best of shape yet, but he won, stopping Davis in the tenth round. The team was happy; they'd come a long way and progress was being made as they continued to work toward changing Buster's training habits.

For the next fight, they fought again for Don King, this time paired against Jerry Halstead, a rugged fighter out of Oklahoma. Buster stopped him in the ninth round. King was a little happier after this fight. It was April 16, 1988.

A couple of months later, on June 27, 1988, Buster was to fight Mike Williams in Atlantic City on the Mike Tyson–Michael

Spinks undercard—a major fight for the Douglas team. Don King had just given Williams, an up-and-coming, undefeated fighter out of Texas, a $50,000 bonus to sign with him. Johnson smiles as he recalls J. D. McCauley saying that Buster Douglas won every fight that Don King wanted him to lose and lost every fight that Don King wanted him to win.

Johnson knew that this was a fight King expected them to lose. They'd just come off a less than sterling performance against Halstead and the fact that King signed Williams to such a substantial bonus was meaningful. Buster dominated the fight, knocking Williams down three times with his left jab—people who saw it still talk about it. Buster ultimately stopped him in the seventh round with a combination of punches, but the machine-gun jabs were the highlight of the fight. And those jabs would ultimately be the difference in Tokyo.

When asked, Johnson says that Buster's three greatest fights were Greg Page, Mike Williams, and, of course, Mike Tyson. He takes great pride in the fact that from the Tucker fight on Buster never lost a fight and believes strongly that the physical and mental motivation he and J. D. were supplying resulted in the eventual string of victories.

Six months after the Williams fight Buster would be facing Trevor Berbick in Las Vegas. Johnson recalls that during this period of Buster's career they were lucky to work with some of the top cut men in the business. Johnny Tacco would be with them in the corner for the Berbick fight, and they also worked with Billy Prezant and Eddie Aliano on several occasions. Johnson says he learned a great deal from these unmatched professionals.

The Berbick fight, set for February 25, 1989, would be on the Tyson-Bruno undercard. Looking back on Buster's career, he had been fortunate to fight on some outstanding undercards, linked forever to great championship fights. For example, he fought under Larry Holmes during his title run. Johnson considers Larry Holmes, Buster Douglas, and Muhammad Ali to possess the most lethal jabs of any heavyweight who ever stepped into the ring. Of course, in Johnson's eyes one fighter will always rank above the rest, Muhammad Ali. Ali transcends the very sport itself. "Here is a man working to create love and understanding between all nations." Johnson says. "If only our leaders would stop and listen to his words the world would be a far better place." Looking back on his life, Johnson's says the only thing that rivals Tokyo is the fact that he was touched directly by Muhammad Ali.

Back to February 25, 1989, Las Vegas, Nevada, and Trevor Berbick. It wasn't the perfect performance Johnson was so desperately looking for, but Buster took Berbick in a 10-round decision. Johnson and the team were basically pleased with the win but Johnson wanted more. In fact, until the Tyson fight Johnson will tell you he was never satisfied.

After the Berbick win Don King called again. It would be Oliver McCall on July 21, 1989, with the winner getting a shot at world champion Mike Tyson. The team went into high gear, immediately stepping up the training as everyone was pumped at the opportunity for the world's attention. Then, out of the blue, Buster announced to his team that he didn't want to fight. Johnson says he'll never forget the startling moment—they'd all been working so hard and now, right in the middle of it all, Buster was ready to call it quits. In the middle of his training, his hands still wrapped, he walked over to the steps beside the ring, sat down next to Johnson, and said, "I don't want to fight; I'm not going to fight."

Johnson was worried that he'd been pressing Buster too hard and that the harsh words he'd leveled at his fighter to keep him focused had driven him over the edge. Johnson told Buster that they needed to talk, privately. They walked over to an empty indoor soccer field in their training facility and sat down. Looking back, Johnson believes Buster was scared—the kind of fear that can grip an athlete when he knows he's getting close to the dream. Johnson told Buster it was simply out of the question for him to quit now, with so many people counting on him and his dream so close to becoming a reality. He told Buster that he had no doubt that he would beat McCall and that Tyson would go down in the title fight. Buster didn't respond. The next day Johnson set up a meeting with their attorney, Steve Enz, thinking it would help put things in perspective for Buster. Steve Enz had been with them since the Tucker fight, drawing up their first contract and basically keeping them out of any legal distractions. Johnson remembers his first meeting with Enz when he told him that he had no money to pay him for his services, but when the money followed Buster's success he had Johnson's word that he would be paid. Enz agreed to those terms and a longstanding relationship began. Buster respected Steve Enz and Johnson knew that whatever he had to say would carry more weight if Steve backed him up. So they double-teamed Buster in Steve's office that day, both telling him that it was this fight or it was over for him. Johnson threw a hat he had just bought with "Only My Best—James Douglas" in the trash can and said he was done. James then changed his mind and said he was going to fight.

In preparation for the McCall fight, Douglas and his team arrived early in Atlantic City, New Jersey. This bout would be the undercard of the Mike Tyson and Carl "The Truth" Williams championship fight. Johnson and Douglas were pumped. Johnson recalls watching Buster running the boardwalk and sprinting on the beach every morning. Those 10 days leading up to the fight were some of Buster's best training days. Buster would win a 10-round decision over McCall, but it was another lackluster performance by Buster—Johnson did not want to think about what would have happened to his fighter if he fought in the same manner against the seemingly indestructible Mike Tyson.

The time had arrived. After six long years and many dark nights, the lives of John Johnson and James "Buster" Douglas were about to take on a new and irreversible aspect. Fame was now lurking next to the two men from Columbus, Ohio, the two men who grew up in as different an environment as could be imagined. They would travel together now to the other side of the planet in search of their new destiny. Fame and fortune indeed had been their dream and now only time would tell where the journey would lead.

King had initially assured Johnson that the fight would be held sometime in October. The Douglas team decided it best to take a full week off after the McCall fight and then begin training for the world title. But sometime in September King informed Johnson of a change in plans. The fight would have to be delayed. King had set up a bout between Tyson and Razor Ruddock instead and Douglas would again fight the undercard against Ken Lakusta. But destiny wouldn't have it. Tyson was injured during his training for Ruddock, opening the door for Douglas as originally planned when Ruddock couldn't commit to the new fight date.

It was back to full training for Buster. Now the Columbus press began to show interest in their new hometown celebrity. Johnson fondly remembers a prime-time television spot that was shot in Columbus showing Buster running at 5 A.M. in Sharon Woods Park with icicles hanging off his sweaty face. Again, Johnson brought in new blood to test Buster and prepare him for the biggest test of his life. He hired three young, very tough sparring partners. James Pritchard out of Louisville, Kentucky, Greg Whitaker out of North Carolina, and Young Joe Louis out of Chicago were all about the same size as Tyson and had been taught to emulate the champ's fighting style for this particular sparring period. They would all arrive several months before the fight so Buster could work against fresh opponents every two or three rounds during the entire training period. Johnson would later praise these three young fighters for their outstanding work that meant so much to the team's later success in Tokyo.

Johnson would be stepping into a new world when he began his contract negotiations with King. King invited Johnson to his training compound in the countryside south of Cleveland, Ohio, to talk about the Tokyo fight and finalize the deal. Johnson, sensing that he would need all the support he could get, brought along his good friend Red Banks. They stopped on the way outside of East Cleveland—Shaker Heights—and picked up another friend, a former Ohio State football player, Ron Springs. Springs had been an outstanding tailback for Woody Hayes, and Johnson had been active in recruiting him out of high school. The two stayed friends after their days as Buckeyes. "This was a case where Ron Springs could've been one of the great tailbacks in Ohio State history," Johnson talks passionately about his friend. "But he got caught up in a situation where he didn't really get the opportunity he should've." Ron Springs represents so many players that come out of the Ohio State football program, and other systems like Ohio State, players who get to the edge of greatness only to see their young lives' plans and dreams pass them by. There are all kinds of reasons why this happens (some out of control of the athlete) to these young men. Athletes can have the ability, the right mind-set, and put in the proper amount of study and training and still not reach their ultimate goals. The odds are just so difficult. Ron Springs had it all, and although he did have an outstanding career at Ohio State, with a few breaks and perhaps different coaching decisions he could've been among the elite of the Ohio State football alumni. John Johnson's football instincts were correct again as Ron Springs's outstanding NFL career would prove. For reasons Johnson only sensed, he wanted his two friends with him that unforgettable day in the countryside outside of Cleveland.

The term "negotiation" doesn't quite describe the meeting that occurred between Johnson and King in preparation for the fight. It was a delicate situation for Johnson especially. If you think about it, Johnson wasn't exactly in a position of strength in dealing with King. It wasn't like Douglas was a number-one contender for the title, plus there were hundreds of fighters who would be eager to trade places with Buster and fight for the world title. So you couldn't say Johnson was in a position to play hardball with King. In the end, Johnson would play his hand nearly perfectly. King agreed to pay Buster Douglas $1.3 million, including an extra $100,000 bonus should Buster defeat Tyson, thus taking away his heavyweight title (this bonus clause would become an important element of the contract after the fight). To put this deal in proper perspective, the most Johnson and Douglas received for any fight up to this point was $250,000, for the Tucker fight.

Johnson tells a revealing story concerning Don King and the contract negotiations. Johnson was walking the property with King after their meeting and while standing next to a pond Johnson told King he would have to get final approval for the deal from Buster before he could accept the offer. King grabbed Johnson's arm and said, "Now, Johnny, don't be like that dog that's got a bone in his mouth and looks into the water and suddenly sees a bigger bone in the water and he drops the one in his mouth to jump into the water after it. John, you think hard about the bucks in your hand."

Johnson would learn many lessons while on his path to the title. For example, Johnson almost hired Richie Giachetti to be the cut man for the fight. Later in a book Giachetti actually took credit for teaching Buster his great jab, the jab that floored Mike Williams three times in one round, the jab that kept Mike Tyson from getting inside on Buster in Tokyo. The real truth, according to Johnson, is that one man and one man only taught Buster how to fight, his father "Dynamite" Bill Douglas. Johnson goes back further and explains that Bill Douglas learned his boxing trade from Ed Williams—Coach Ed Williams as he respectfully calls him. Johnson claims that Coach Williams taught them all. He insists that Williams was the best trainer to ever come out of Columbus, Ohio.

A cut man named John Russell would eventually be hired by Johnson to be in the corner in Tokyo. So it would be J. D. McCauley as head trainer, John Russell as the cut man, and a young group of sparring partners who joined Johnson as the final team that would surround Buster for the big fight. This was the team that Johnson put together and Johnson insists on calling it a team. "Everyone on this team performed beyond my expectations," he said. Johnson believes in his heart that if this team would have stayed intact and kept the same desire, dedication, and determination, Douglas would have defeated Evander Holyfield and Mike Tyson in the rematch, and would have been considered one of the greatest fighters of all time. Johnson quickly reminds anyone around him that if you don't believe in the importance of the team concept with respect to boxing, just ask the man of boxing himself, Angelo Dundee.

James and John were scheduled to fly to Los Angeles three weeks before their flight to Tokyo for a prefight press conference. It would be the last time Johnson would see Buster's mom alive. Johnson remembers the moment as if it happened yesterday—he picked up Buster to go to the airport and there was Lula Pearl mopping the kitchen floor with a huge smile on her face. From the first day Johnson met her she made him feel like part of the family. No mother was prouder of her boy than Lula Pearl Douglas. Johnson recalls driving to the airport that day. Buster discovered that he'd forgotten his dress shirt for the press conference so Johnson called his cousin Paul Lemley, who rushed to a local men's store to pick up a shirt for Buster. The press conference was a special time for Johnson because Buster publicly expressed his deep gratitude for Johnson's mentoring and for sticking by him during difficult times. Johnson and Buster flew back to Columbus after the press conference and two days later Johnson got the call from J. D. that Lula Pearl had passed.

Johnson asked Buster if he wanted him to cancel or postpone the fight. Without a moment's hesitation Buster said no, his mom wouldn't want him to do that, she knew how much the fight meant to her boy. That best sums up Lula Pearl's love for her son. Johnson and Buster would leave for Tokyo immediately after the funeral. Much has been said about the effect of James's mother's death on the fight itself. Johnson would add that without question, James's inspiration in that ring came directly form his mom.

It would be an early morning flight out of Columbus and Johnson noted that only one local Columbus news station met them at the gate. Doug Lesells from Channel 4 News greeted the two. They were headed for Tokyo for the world heavyweight title against a man who many were referring to as the greatest fighter of our time and only one local television station showed. Lesells shoved the microphone at Johnson and asked, "John, you're getting ready to go to Tokyo, Buster's fighting Mike Tyson, what are your thoughts right now?" Without hesitation Johnson said, "We're going to Tokyo and Buster Douglas is not only going to beat Mike Tyson, he's going to knock him out!"

They had a short layover in Chicago and then a 13-hour flight to Japan. Johnson didn't believe a plane could stay in the air that long. When Johnson saw the island of Japan he thought he was in a movie. The team arrived 16 days before the fight. Johnson felt very strange and out of place there. The time change, the long flight, the people, it all didn't seem real to him. The night that they arrived he didn't get a minute's sleep; he felt the weight of the world on his shoulders.

It would be a good week on the ground before they started feeling even close to normal. The Japanese had the two boxers participate in public workouts. Tyson would work out first and then Douglas. Buster did not look sharp in the early workouts. He was slow and lethargic. The public workouts were constantly full of people, maybe 500 or more, nothing like the tiny, empty training space in Columbus. After one of the workouts Johnson tracked down the Japanese promoter, Mr. Akihiko Honda. Johnson promised him that Buster would be ready for the fight, that what he saw in the ring was not the real Buster Douglas. The Japanese official gave Johnson a gracious Japanese smile and a quick bow; Johnson thought the guy didn't believe a word he was saying.

Three days before the fight Buster got sick. He called Johnson at 7 A.M. and sounded like death. Johnson thought they would have to actually cancel the fight. They were staying at the Grand Palace Hotel and there was a doctor in residence. The doctor shot Buster full of penicillin, and gave him a jar full of antibiotics. Johnson cut back the training and just hoped for the best. Johnson remembers like it was yesterday, the day before the fight Buster, as Johnson describes it, "shook out" in front of the hotel lobby elevators and started shadow boxing right there. Johnson never saw Buster look better. And he remembered the story of young Buster Douglas watching his father shadow boxing in the locker room after one of his fights. The son was ready.

5

TYSON

I'm just a dark guy from the den of iniquity, a shadowy figure from the bowels of iniquity.

—Mike Tyson

Mike Tyson's mother wasn't in the ring with him that fateful afternoon in Tokyo, Japan. Some demons we carry can be overcome. Some demons can be ignored and put away, hidden for a lifetime. Others stay with you like a bad dream that will never end. Michael Gerald Tyson was born on June 30, 1966, in Brooklyn, New York. Michael's father left his son and mother when Mike was young. Soon mother and son moved to Brownsville (in the heart of Brooklyn) a place that can only be described as a living hell. When Tyson was just a boy he woke one day to find his favorite pet pigeon, Julius, dead. He was devastated. In honor of his dead friend young Tyson decided to use part of the bird's crate as a stickball bat. Tyson describes what happened. "I left the crate on my stoop and went inside to get something. I returned to see the sanitation man putting the crate into the crusher. I rushed him and caught him flush on the temple with a titanic right hand, he was out cold, convulsing on the ground like an infantile retard." And so Mike Tyson began his decent into retribution justice. "I'm just a dark guy from a den of iniquity, a shadowy figure from the bowels of iniquity. I wish I could be Mike who gets endorsement deals. But you can't make a lie and a truth go together. This country wasn't built on moral fiber. This country was built on rape, slavery, murder, degradation, and affiliation with crime."

Buster Douglas carried the memory of his mother with him into the ring in Tokyo, Japan. Tyson carried fear, hatred, and pain. Mike Tyson could attack most of his demons with his fists. But how does a fatherless young man from the streets of Brooklyn come to grips with the emptiness of life with a mother he does not know, a mother who did not want to know her own son.

Mike Tyson joined the Jolly Stompers when he was 10 years old. We know now that the gangs roaming our large cities are much more complex than we once believed. These aren't just kids looking to have some fun after school. Gangs may represent many things, but clearly one undeniable reality we must recognize is the desperate search for family that these kids, mostly young men, are seeking. Why this quest often turns to violence is a deep question for another story. But clearly, 10-year-old Mike Tyson was a poster child for the gang life.

The Jolly Stompers came calling because of another dead pigeon. As a young, shy boy, Tyson's only friends were his pigeons. Tyson's relationship with pigeons and other animals would continue throughout his life. He was nine years old when he met his first gang member. The meeting would change Tyson's life forever. The 15-year-old grabbed one of Tyson's pigeons. Mike pleaded with the local gang member to give it back only to watch him slowly twist the bird's head until it snapped. Nine-year-old Mike Tyson flew into a rage. Local eyewitnesses would later describe the resulting attack as an unrelenting massacre. Word quickly spread to the gangs in Brownsville; a new enforcer was in town.

The next three years would lead to the bottom of an already spiraling life. A blinding series of assaults, burglaries, and muggings was followed by a series of incarcerations. First was the Spofford Juvenile Detention Center where Tyson had an accidental encounter with Muhammad Ali. Ali was visiting the center and Tyson may had experienced the first gleam of a dream when he saw Ali. But it wouldn't be until Tyson was 13 that the reality of boxing began to take shape.

After a particularly brutal assault Tyson was sent to the Tryon School in upstate New York. Due to a continued inability to conform, he spent much of his time at the school handcuffed and in solitary confinement. And then the change began. One day Tyson asked his counselor if he could meet Bobby Stewart. Stewart was a former boxer who was now a boxing instructor at the Tryon School. After some tough negotiations Stewart agreed to work with Tyson. Finally, after a lifetime of darkness 13-year-old Mike Tyson finally felt hope. It was a simple deal; young Tyson must reverse his abhorrent behavior and start hitting the books, and in exchange Stewart would begin to train Tyson in the art of boxing. Mike Tyson's life would never be the same.

After only a few lessons it was clear to Stewart he had stumbled across a once-in-a-lifetime talent. Meanwhile, Tyson became obsessed with his new world. Nothing else mattered to the troubled man-boy. Alongside his intense physical training he began to study the history of the sport. He read everything he could get his hands on concerning past boxing champions. He studied their lives and their ring boxing techniques. Tyson had finally become a student. But soon the student would outgrow the teacher. Stewart quickly realized he needed to move Tyson up the boxing ladder. Enter the legendary Cus D'Amato.

If there was ever a young man in need of a father figure it was Mike Tyson. If there was ever an older man in need of a young protégé it was Cus D'Amato. Pulitzer Prize winning author Norman Mailer called D'Amato a Zen master. Muhammad Ali all but begged him to be his trainer. And he was the man who directed the career of Floyd Patterson. But D'Amato was 20 years removed from the peak of his boxing heights by the time Mike Tyson entered the New York reformatory system. D'Amato had been living in the Catskills training local boxing talent and anyone else who stumbled into his gym above the Catskills Police Station. Stewart not only stumbled into D'Amato's gym he actually climbed into the ring with Tyson to help demonstrate the young man's potential. Stewart had hoped that if D'Amato would see his boy fight six or seven times he just might take the kid on. To his astonishment, after Stewart and Tyson traded blows for only three rounds, D'Amato had seen enough. He pulled Stewart to the side and whispered, "The kid's a future world champion if he wants it bad enough."

 **6**

CUS

If it weren't for Mike Tyson, I wouldn't be alive.
                                                    —Cus D'Amato

Cus D'Amato was dead. He was still breathing and walking around, but he was dead. He would have told you so himself. Cus D'Amato was 20 years removed from the eye of the professional boxing world and buried in upstate New York. He was 77 years old and still breathing . . . and dead. But D'Amato was about to learn the true meaning of life after death. It was to come in the surprising specter of Mike Tyson.

Constantine "Cus" D'Amato was a living legend in the world of boxing. His life is what movies are made of. Born the seventh of eight sons to an Italian immigrant in the Fog Hollow section of the Bronx, Cus D'Amato personally understood the harsh nature of the boxing underworld. In fact, D'Amato helped shape it. But his "boxing" training began long before he had even a hint at the realities of the business.

Cus learned about pain from his father. But unlike most kids, his reaction to being beaten with a whip to be kept in line was pure D'Amato, "It only meant I would never be intimidated by the threat of pain later." This was the man who, while serving in the armed forces, would voluntarily step up his own punishment in the face of his superior officers. Private D'Amato was ordered to stand at attention for two hours, but young D'Amato instead would stand for three. And D'Amato would never consider "working" for anyone. Cus D'Amato *assisted* the people in the streets, the people he grew up with. He acted as a street consigliore,

resolving disputes between locals and insurance companies re-
fusing to make good on claims, or local shysters who had taken
fees and not provided promised services. He never took money
for these acts—expenses, or other forms of quid pro quo, yes, if it
fit his needs and ethics. This was the way he felt comfortable
doing business, the old way.

And this was how he got his famed work place, the Gramercy
Gym. D'Amato learned that an old friend, a friend with money,
wanted to get into the filling station business. D'Amato went to
City Hall and pored over maps and public hearing documents
and learned that a new road, Bruckner Boulevard, was about to
be built right through the Bronx. He quietly passed the informa-
tion on to his friend who bought up the land and built five filling
stations along the proposed route. The friend made a fortune.
D'Amato didn't take a dime. But later the same friend learned
that D'Amato wanted to buy a local gymnasium and train fighters. He staked D'Amato and the Gramercy Gym was born. But to
refer to the Gramercy as simply a gym is like calling Yankee Stadium just a baseball park. The Gramercy was Cus D'Amato's
living laboratory; D'Amato didn't just train young fighters, he
trained young men. It was never just boxing for D'Amato, it was
always teaching life. Cus D'Amato said, "Kids growing up in a
rough neighborhood have to go through a number of experiences
in life that are intimidating and embarrassing. These experiences
form layer upon layer over their capabilities and talents. My job
as a teacher is to peel off these layers."

D'Amato's theories and street philosophy would be put to
the ultimate test in 1949. A Chicago millionaire, James D. Norris
Jr., decided to corner the market of the boxing industry. He formed
a consortium with a simple but brilliant plan. The International
Boxing Club (IBC) would buy off the current world champion,
Joe Louis, for $150,000 forcing him to announce his retirement.
At the same time Norton and his group purchased the contracts of
the remaining top four heavyweight contenders. The IBC went
on through the divisions of professional boxing, buying up the
talent in each division, until it controlled virtually every fighter

in the country. The perfect crime was nearly complete. But Norton and company hadn't counted on Cus D'Amato. D'Amato had been training for this fight his whole life. Instinctively, D'Amato knew how to beat these guys—with patience and the right fighter. "I couldn't fight them alone," D'Amato would later say, "I needed to wait for the perfect fighter to fight them with, a kid who not only had great talent but was loyal. If he was a talent but not loyal, it wouldn't do me any good, I needed a special kid." That kid would be Floyd Patterson.

In 1952 Floyd Patterson won the gold medal in the Helsinki Olympics. Patterson was 17 years old. But D'Amato had discovered Patterson when he was 14 and just out of the Wiltwick School for Boys, a school for disturbed children in Esopus, New York. Sound familiar? For three years D'Amato trained the kid. He worked him in the ring and he worked him outside the ring. "He was a good kid. He was game and determined, but most important he was a good kid." D'Amato watched his new young protégé; he studied him until he knew his entire character. "Floyd was the kid to take on the IBC." He was overwhelmingly introverted to the point that a simple conversation left him immobile. D'Amato handled the young fighter like a psychological surgeon. His basic tactic was not to ever criticize or lecture him. D'Amato wouldn't even talk to Floyd directly, but he would speak to a third person within Floyd's earshot. He would talk about his theories of fear and intimidation, slowly molding his fighter's mental toughness. It didn't end there. D'Amato purposely carried himself in a more self-assured way, more animated than his usual personality. He even altered his dress. Normally a casual dresser, D'Amato became an elegant dresser, actually donning a fancy homburg hat. Why this change? He wanted to convey to Patterson that he had nothing to be ashamed of, that he was someone of importance. "I always knew Floyd was watching and listening to me, I never let on, but I always knew."

While he was training Patterson, D'Amato never stopped waiting for the right moment for the big move. The moment arrived in 1956 in the person of Hurricane Jackson. The Hurricane was the IBC's No. 1 contender. Somehow D'Amato managed to match his fighter with the contender. Patterson won a tough decision over Jackson and now the IBC had no choice but to agree to a match with their top man, the revered Archie Moore. Floyd Patterson won in dramatic fashion, knocking out the champ with a leaping left hook in the fifth round. The IBC was reeling. It would be a slow-running death as D'Amato refused to let Patterson fight an IBC-sponsored boxer. The end came when the IBC was declared a monopoly and shut down by the government. The Zen master had struck. It would be another 20 years before he would be back. A reporter would ask an older D'Amato, "What has it meant to be back with Tyson?"

"It's meant everything," D'Amato responded. "If it weren't for Michael, I probably wouldn't be alive, not dead, just not really alive. You see Mother Nature can play strange tricks on us. In our life we develop certain pleasures and certain people we care about. Then nature brutally takes them away, one by one. I believe it's her way of preparing us for death. I didn't have any pleasures left and my friends were all gone, I wasn't hearing things, I wasn't seeing things. Mother Nature was preparing me to die. Then Mike came into my life. I now have the motivation to live. A person dies when he no longer wants to live. He finds a convenient disease, like a fighter who doesn't want to fight finds a convenient corner to lie down. Boxing, life, death."

7

SNOWELL

Muhammad Ali was testing us.

—Aaron Snowell

Aaron Snowell found his way out of the Philadelphia projects. A 12 year old, living with his mom and 10 siblings, he somehow discovered a way to break the seemingly unending cycle of poverty and despair that lives in the inner cities of our great nation. Aaron Snowell found Muhammad Ali. Or more accurately, Ali found Snowell.

Aaron Snowell and his brothers and sisters were invited to Ali's private room while they were visiting his boxing camp in Philadelphia. The kids nervously waited for the already legendary Ali, not knowing what they were doing in his room. Soon Ali joined them. Without saying a word he put a black satchel on the bed and left. The bag was full of cash. The test had begun. Of course Aaron and his young siblings didn't have a clue as they sat frozen, waiting for the larger-than-life Ali to return. After what seemed like a lifetime to Aaron, the door finally banged open and suddenly Ali filled the room again. Ali could see not only that the bag of cash had not been touched, the kids hadn't moved from the very spot in which he had left them. In thinking back on the moment Snowell swears he didn't breath the entire time Ali was gone. "To this day I still can't believe it happened." Snowell drifts off when he talks about his first meeting with Ali, as if he's trying to relive a moment in time that must now seem unreal. "He was testing us. Muhammad Ali was testing 11 little kids from the projects. How about that for an introduction to the world of boxing?

I didn't know it at the time but that was the beginning of a new life for me, a new world."

Aaron Snowell has an irresistible calmness about him. It never leaves the man. Whether he's reflecting on his tumultuous past with Mike Tyson or giving instructions to his fighter in the corner between intense rounds in a heavyweight championship fight, his demeanor never changes. It's a calmness born of confidence, the kind of confidence that can only come from a lifetime of experience in the gym. When Aaron Snowell speaks he speaks with unchallenged authority.

When Mike Tyson hooked up with Aaron Snowell the champ was in trouble. Not with the law, with a woman. Tyson was the undisputed heavyweight champion of the world and his life was in a meltdown. He had demolished 34 consecutive opponents in less than four years. No fighter on the planet had come close to putting Tyson on the canvas. It would take a woman to do that. The woman was Robin Givens. This wasn't a private melt down, but was played out the good old American way, in the press and on national television. (Who can ever forget the shell-shocking *20/20* interview?) Tyson was rudderless and in an uncontrollable spiral when he agreed to move to Don King's remote compound in Southington, Ohio. Enter Snowell. "Mike was sent to me to cut his weight," Snowell reflects. "He tipped the scales at about 315 pounds." When asked how does one begin to approach this task, Snowell, in workmanlike fashion, answers, "Right foods, mind-set, attitude, spirit, the whole package."

Snowell and Tyson weren't strangers. "It was 1987; I was training Julian Jackson at Don King's camp in Ohio," Snowell reflects back. "Julian was a three-time WBA [World Boxing Association] junior middleweight champion. He's a three-time world champ. But Mike and I had a common history. We grew up in the business at the same time. So we crossed paths and talked a lot over the early years. You have to understand, even when he was beating everyone in his path he could walk through the hotels and casinos after a fight and no one would recognize him. He was shy in those days and since we were both young it was easier for

Mike to talk to me." Snowell continues, "So we had a good relationship before he came to Ohio to train with me."

Snowell quickly returns to the subject of Tokyo. "Someone has to take the blame. I can take the failure. But I can also take the successes that we had. It's like this," Snowell holds out his hands. "It's both hands, without the lows there's no highs. All you have to live with is yourself. I trained Tyson back into fighting shape and we beat Frank Bruno in five in Las Vegas, we knocked out Carl 'The Truth' Williams in Atlantic City in one. The following Saturday on the *Wide World of Sports* I had Julian Jackson fight Terry Norris and Jackson knocked Terry Norris out in two rounds. There was good, hard work here." Even when Snowell turns to the problems in Tokyo his steady manner never changes. "There was a cut man in the corner named Taylor Smith. He didn't have all the necessary equipment for the fight. Now, I was the head trainer so it's my responsibility. All of the post-fight talk concerning problems in the corner [the image of what looked like a water-filled balloon pressed against Tyson's swollen face stands out] I'll take the responsibility for that, but Mike was in shape to fight. To me, it was a combination of the following factors that led to the final result in Tokyo. Number one, he was going through a divorce and he was still in love with Robin Givens and wanted to be with her. And like anyone that's going through something like that the mood swings that you have and wanting to be somewhere else, it was too much to overcome. Second, I think if the fight had been in the United States it would've been much different. The Japanese are not people that are in awe. I'll tell you, the day Mike got knocked down sparring with Greg Page was press day and all the media of Tokyo was in the gym. It was like 'bombs away' once he got knocked down. The flashes from all the cameras, it was unbelievable. But personally they're emotionless people, they don't show any emotion. Take the fight itself, it was a great, exciting fight but they showed no excitement. It was total silence. Like I always said, you could hear a rat pissing on cotton it was so quiet in that arena. Mike always responded to the crowd. He was an emotional fighter. The roar of the crowd brings energy to Mike. So the combination of his mind-set going into the fight, and not having the right kind of atmosphere in the arena to over-come his missing Robin, he just wasn't mentally ready. This is not meant to take anything away from Buster. Buster was ready for that fight. But the truth is Mike Tyson didn't want to be in Tokyo."

TOKYO

The hay's in the barn.

—Woody Hayes

It was three o'clock in the morning; John Johnson and his fighting team had arrived in Tokyo earlier that day. Johnson was now curled up in his hotel bed high above the city but sleep was not an option. This is a time when the mind can play with dangerous thoughts. What was he doing in this strange place? In Tokyo, Japan? If only he could see Red Jacket again . . . just one more time. That's where he really belonged, not on the other side of the planet. In a few hours, everything he had visualized since he was a kid in the green hills of mining country would become real— a dream come true—so why the fear? Why was he afraid of the very thing he had planned for his entire life? It can happen. A person can be near enough to a dream to touch it but want only to turn and run. Johnson could now touch his dream. Right there, immobilized in his bed at three in the morning above Tokyo. But that's when doubts enter. Johnson was starting to question everything; maybe he was too far from his home, maybe he didn't belong here. And what of the fight? Was Buster really ready? Was he?

Johnson once overheard Coach Hayes address this very situation. A young quarterback, scared down to his jock just before starting his first game in the Ohio Stadium, made the mistake of telling his coach that he felt frozen, unable to move, that maybe he wasn't ready. The young athlete confided this after completing more training and practice than an average person could even begin to imagine. It was pure fear. And Hayes had seen it before. "You'll get your butt through this son, or, by God, I'll kick it through." Subtlety was not a known trait of Hayes. The young quarterback went out and set a single-game passing record in his first start for the Buckeyes. In the end, it's all about the preparation. That's what gets you through those situations, preparation. In his calmer moments, Hayes would put it another way. Late in any week of practice during the football season, when he sensed his boys were feeling the fear, questioning their confidence as Saturday afternoon approached, he would simply bring the team together and tell them, "Boys, our work is done. The hay's in the barn."

In the end Johnson knew the hay was in the barn for Buster. As the day of the fight loomed closer Johnson believed in his mind and soul he'd prepared his fighter in a way that would make his mentor proud. Johnson had learned from the best and now he was ready for the lessons to pay off and for the dream to come true.

Johnson, reflecting back on Tokyo, says, "the morning of the fight I was in the shower and I felt overwhelmed. I remember saying a short prayer: 'Lord, should we win, I'll never forget.' I've never forgot and I never will. Coach Hayes always said you don't pay back, you pay forward and that's exactly what I believe. We all should share our good fortunes with those in need."

As the team was waiting in the locker room before being called out to the arena, Johnson believed that Buster was going to make Tyson quit before the fight went the scheduled 12 rounds. He thought Buster would pound on him for six or seven rounds and Tyson would just finally quit. He was wrong. Johnson gained great respect for Mike Tyson during the fight. He fought his heart out and no one can tell Johnson to his face that Tyson wasn't in shape and ready to fight. "You don't take a whipping like that for 10 rounds and not be in great shape physically. Now mentally, I don't think Tyson really believed he was ever going to be in a battle. James changed that."

❐ ❑ ❐

The Prefight Tokyo Press Conference

The word "upset" is more significant in boxing than any other sport, it hovers over the ring at all times. Anytime two men weighing over 200 pounds get in the ring anything can happen.

—Don King

The Don King Tokyo show had begun. It kicked off in Los Angeles, California, with HBO representative Seth Abraham opening the press conference in front of a huge Home Box Office banner. "Good morning everybody, and welcome to Home Box Office. My name is Seth Abraham, and I rarely have the opportunity to introduce Don King. It generally goes the other way around. Thank you for joining us. We've called this a 'Sayonara Breakfast' or 'Sayonara Reception.' Most of you know now that Mike and Buster are leaving for Tokyo this morning or early this afternoon for the February 10–February 11 in Tokyo—Home Box Office championship prize fight.

"I don't have much to say other than nothing draws like a heavyweight championship fight. Home Box Office has been doing fights since 1972, going back to the reign of Ali; and in terms of important programming for Home Box Office, nothing is as good as a heavyweight championship fight. You add to that Mike Tyson, and you have a major league event. Also, I do not discount Buster Douglas; he has fought several times on Home Box Office, and we are delighted to have him matched up against the heavyweight champ.

"Before I turn this over to the real principals, because we're not really principals in that sense, we have a little gift for some of the people who are going away. As you all know, Mike comes into the ring without a robe. Of course, it is tradition or legendary for the Japanese, the great warriors, the sumo wrestlers, the samurai, to go in robes, so we thought we would give Mike and Buster and Don samurai robes. When they were given to me, I saw that they had Japanese characters on them. I thought it might be interesting if I knew exactly what it said on the robe before I presented it to the men. It says, '*Long live a long life.*' So with that I'll turn it over to Don King." Mr. Abraham hands a gift box to the three. "Mike, a robe for you; and Buster, a robe for you."

Don King: Open it up, Buster and put it on. We'll be in style going to the land of the Rising Sun. Destination: Tokyo—with our samurai robes on.

[*The press starts taking pictures of the fighters putting on their robes.*]

Seth Abraham: I want you to note that these heavyweight robes are perfect fits.

Don King: I'm a smaller sumo wrestler. [*Don King's robe is a very tight fit*]

Ladies and gentlemen, as I said earlier, this is a very important day for us to be taking off for Tokyo, Japan, to fight in the Korakuen Arena in Tokyo.

Today is Martin Luther King's birthday; he would be 61 years old today. The whole nation is paying homage to him. It is really an important situation because he is the first that [*sic*] would get a national holiday, Martin Luther King. And he died for us in effect of trying to make America a better and brighter place, preaching togetherness—unity and solidarity and togetherness. And in so doing, he was the apostle of peace and therefore the nation is going to honor him today. I understand that at 12 o'clock noon today they will ring the Liberty Bell in Philadelphia. This is important for us as a class of people, and black people; and it is important for the nation that they will begin to recognize us as making contributions to this great land. I love America and I love the American people. I think this is the greatest nation in the world. And it makes me proud when I see them begin to be exemplary of the profound statement that they have in their constitution: "That we hold these truths to be self-evident, that all men are created equal, endowed by the creator with certain unalienable rights, among these which are life, liberty and the pursuit of happiness." I think that's important that we should adhere to that and continue to work toward making it become a living reality in this great land of ours.

We are going to have a prizefight in Tokyo. This is a "Sayonara Breakfast" this morning at HBO, the network of champions. You've seen the heavyweight champion on his own and the man who introduced me on the sidelines there if you've seen this month's *Sports Illustrated*, a young genius that's working out on the field of sports in boxing, a young Jewish lad who happened to be born on the same day that I was on [*sic*], only a few years difference. We both have the same birthday, so it's more than prophetic in our relationship that many people try to find out what happened, how did it happen, when did it happen, but this is a normal thing for people that are gifted. I'm young, gifted, and black; and he's young, gifted, and white, and so we're showing that working together works. To play a piano and have a concerto by the greatest of the impresarios in the world, the greatest concert pianists have to play the black keys as well as the white keys to get the notes out to make it feel good, so to your ears it'll be pleasing (ebony and ivory). From the font of Tchaikovsky, Chopin, Brahms, Bach, and Beethoven come Seth Abraham and Don King and HBO.

So it's a thrill for me to be going, and I want you to meet and greet these guys. They're going to say a few words to you as we take off for the airport for Japan Airlines. Buster will be going in a week or so

and coming over. So for those of you in Japan,
"*Nippon Ichiban.*" We want you to know that we are
going over there and we are driving our Toyotas.
They've got Toyotas waiting on us. We've got
Lexuses here that we drive, but my friend Max won't
leave his Ford Mustang, so they said they will have
Ford Mustangs for us waiting in Tokyo so that we
can continue to enjoy the sweetness of life that we
do here in America.

So we are thrilled to be able to go over there and
have a good time, and we're gonna have a big fight,
and, naturally, Buster Douglas is going to try to make
history. He's going to try to upset this champion. He
is in really very good shape; he looks very good. John
Johnson has done a magnificent job of encouraging
and motivating him into working hard and persever-
ing. I want to commend you both, John and Buster,
because I think HBO is going to have a helluva fight
on its hands right there in Korakuen Stadium. And,
of course, the immutable, incomparable champion
who is the undefeated, undisputed heavyweight
champion of the world, the baddest man on planet
earth, the baddest man in the universe, is going to try
to continue his reign.

There's one further thing I can say. Right now
we have a great creative genius in directing and producing movies, a man that is far beyond his time,
he's so visionary. And I think that he is one who
implements what he believes. He practices what he
preaches, and his word is gold. Mike Tyson just yesterday said, "That Larry Gordon is a really good guy."
Well, Larry Gordon's had the pleasure and the privi-
lege of signing us up to do a movie. So we got the
contracts—ask Seth Abraham—we got our contracts,
he's representing us, so we're going to be under the
auspices and direction of the great Larry Gordon.

Larry Gordon would you come up here a minute, please? This is our movie director. This guy here has made some fantastic movies. His reputation precedes him. You know, this is our guy; he's the only one that could get me and Mike Tyson to sign a contract together for a movie. Many have come at us from all kinds of ways, but this is our man, Larry Gordon. Say a couple of words, Larry.

Larry Gordon: I didn't know this was going to happen, I want my lawyer. I won't say a darn word. I'll take on Tyson but not King.

Don King: Oh, my god! Oh, no! Oh, man! Okay, come on Buster, say something . . . what have you got to contribute to us right away 'cause we ain't got much time. But, seriously, Buster, come up here and say a few words to the gentlemen and ladies of the press here in Los Angeles. This is a great city, Los Angeles.

Buster Douglas: I'd like to thank you for having me here, and I'd like to thank HBO for giving me another opportunity to fight for the heavyweight championship of the world. I'd also like to take time out to give a great tribute to John Johnson, the man that stood behind me from the beginning. When nobody else believed in me, he was the man that was there, encouraging me that I could do all the things that I had set out to do. All I had to do was to put my mind and effort together, and it would all come about. And it has. It has been a great journey with John."

Reporter: Not to give it away, but what do you have to do to beat Mike?

Buster Douglas: Well, as I said before, the main thing is just to . . . I have to be in the best shape that I have ever been in to be able to do all the things it will take to defeat Mike. For as long as it takes—if it takes 10 or 12 rounds or sooner, that's the main objective, that James Douglas will get in the best shape he can possibly be in so he can go as long as he has to.

Reporter: James, what do you weigh now and what do you expect to come in as?

Buster Douglas: I should come in under 224 pounds. Right now, I'm around 230 pounds. My training has been doing well; I have been getting the best sparring. I feel great. I'm looking forward to an exciting fight. I'm really looking forward to this challenge. And everything has been going great for James Douglas.

Don King: Is there a question for James "Buster" Douglas? Thank you, James. Thank you so much, James.

And now for a man of few words but a lot of power, a guy who I love and you love; and he's a tremendous champion. But before I do, I'd like to introduce the guy he's hugging over there who's one of our family, John Horne. John, stand up a minute— team Tyson.

Let me bring up the champion of the world, a guy who doesn't discriminate on any opponent; he takes them all. He has been the hallmark for HBO. He's really been a guy that's really making it happen, Mike Tyson, the heavyweight champion of the world.

Mike Tyson: I'm happy to take a long trip to defend my title in Japan. I look forward to doing a lot of business with Nippon television again. After it's over, I look forward to coming back to the United States as a champion again. Thank you very much.

Don King: Any questions for the champ?

Reporter: How did you learn to fight? How do you feel? Do you feel that you're in good shape right now?

Mike Tyson: I'm in great shape to fight right now.

Reporter: In the past you said that no one could beat you. Do you still feel that way?

Mike Tyson: Oh, absolutely. Absolutely.

Reporter: Does it get to be boring after a while? I mean, you think there are no contenders, but there's gotta be somebody out there.

Mike Tyson: No, it's never boring, especially when I draw blood. Never.

Reporter: Got that one right. Mike, is there anyone out there who will give you a fight?

Mike Tyson: Well, I'm sure there are guys out there that will give me a fight, but my objective is to win. Everybody knows there's always number two and number three and number four and guys who'll give a helluva show, but they didn't wind up champ. That's my objective, to stay champ. I'm in great shape, especially in my career.

Reporter: How do you stay motivated, Mike?

Mike Tyson: I want to win. Just the same as if you're in school and you get all A's, you want to get all A pluses if you're competitive. I want to be the best that I possibly can be.

Reporter: Are you looking forward to Holyfield?

Mike Tyson: I'm looking forward to taking care of Buster Douglas.

Reporter: Are you studying any of Buster's fights on video?

Mike Tyson: No, I'm not. I never look at anybody's fights.

Reporter: How come?

Mike Tyson: Because I'm confident that no one can beat me so I don't have to watch them fight.

Don King: Thank you, thank you very much. You know, it's very interesting, when people ask about whether there's an opponent or not an opponent. My experience has been that there are always opponents. The word "upset" is more significant in boxing than in any other sport because boxing is unpredictable. It hovers over the ring at all times because anytime two men get in the ring weighing over 200 pounds, anything can happen. In other sports you can call a time-out and send in a substitute. If you run out of gas, there's no gas station in sight. You've got to be able to deal with it and fight. So when you do that, it's like a virtuoso being played on a Stradivarius violin. So I think there are always challengers because yesterday's nobody is tomorrow's somebody. You have to understand that everyone who ever came to any champion or any fight, they always had that in mind when they were born, when their parents birthed them. The pursuit of excellence is what we're really talking about. We all work so very hard to pursue excellence, and excellence is our forte.

We are very happy to be leaving for Tokyo. We love the Japanese people, and we are going over there to see them O-H-I-O. So we'll be talking to them and living with them for the next 30 days. When we come back, we'll be ready to go off to better and greener grounds.

Any more questions?

It has been a delight to have you at the HBO screening room. I want to you to know that HBO is number one in sports. We're big and getting bigger. So the thing is that we're just excited about being here, and the HBO family greets you with this Sayonara Breakfast. We're now going to where you buy Camels at $50 and coffee at $15. Think how wonderful it is here in America. Thank you very much.

PREFIGHT

He was their great little big man.

—John Johnson

As Johnson stood outside the locker room before the fight he felt he was in a different world. He *was* in a different world. Suddenly a voice interrupted his thoughts. "Coach, I can't believe your demeanor, your confidence. You seem to believe without question that Buster Douglas will beat Mike Tyson." Johnson looked up and standing next to him was Joe Theismann. Halfway around the world in a building they call "The Egg" and Johnson's talking to the one and only Joe Theismann. Johnson smiled and forcefully stated, "If Mike Tyson comes out of that other dressing room and gets in the ring, Buster Douglas is going to kick his ass." He was that confident. As Johnson went back into the dressing room he thought, "When this is over Joe Theismann will think I'm a great coach."

The Douglas team was called to the ring. Johnson talks about the rush that you feel while walking up to the ring before a heavyweight title fight—it's impossible to describe, he says. But in Johnson's case he had an extra boost. His daughter, Mary Bevins, loved to sing, and like a typical proud father he believes his daughter has a special voice. Johnson hired songwriter Garth Nutter in Columbus to write a song for his daughter to record for the fight. So it was a double thrill for Johnson as he walked out to that ring with Buster Douglas, the soon to be heavyweight champion, to the voice of his daughter singing *Win It All*. Johnson felt as if he could touch the ceiling of the Egg at that very moment. If you look at any tape of that fight and watch both fighters and their team come into the ring you can see the difference. Larry Merchant, HBO announcer, saw it. Anyone looking closely could see who really wanted to be there that afternoon.

Of course, for Johnson and Douglas it was like an eternity before the fight began. They both would watch a strange scene happen in the ring before the fight as a Japanese man tried to give something to Mike Tyson. Tyson completely ignored him. Johnson understood that Tyson was some kind of hero to the Japanese people; as he likes to say, "He was their great little big man."

Finally, the fight began and just as the team planned it was Buster who was in complete control in the ring. One of the things Johnson is most proud of was a special punch he added just for this fight. He called it, "the stick." It's like a hook only straighter and quicker. Johnson trained Buster to throw "the stick" before Tyson threw his punches. Johnson felt if Buster kept his ass down, stayed in a good leverage position, and threw hard straight punches, with the advantage of his reach, Tyson would be taken out of his normal fight. Buster followed Johnson's instructions to perfection. "That first round was so important for us to win," Johnson says reflecting back. "And James most definitely won it. That first round set the tone for the whole fight."

In a phone interview Joe Theismann reflects back to that memorable afternoon in Japan. "I'd flown to Tokyo to cover a preseason exhibition football game for ESPN. I remember thinking what a bonus to be able to take in a heavyweight championship fight. I'd seen Tyson fight, but didn't even know who Buster Douglas was. Tyson liked to finish people off early," Theismann begins as he describes his take on the fight. "What struck me early in the fight was Buster's ability to take Tyson's punches. I remember so clearly, I could actually see it in Buster's eyes, he realized he could stay with Tyson, punch for punch. I think that was the key for Buster, he knew he had a chance to beat this guy. After that you could see his confidence grow round by round. Honestly, I found myself really rooting for Buster."

When remembering the post-fight, Theismann says, "I had no credentials for the fight. After the fight I found myself standing around outside Buster's dressing room with Donald Trump. Trump had no credentials either. Suddenly we found ourselves jumping over a barrier and being led into Buster's dressing room. It was such a strange feeling; we were all celebrating and embracing each other like we knew everyone in the room. Part of it, I believe, was being in such a foreign place. I've never forgotten that gesture, John Johnson and his son John II, letting us in that locker room. It was simply an unforgettable sporting event for me."

RINGSIDE

Oh, about ninety seconds.
> —Ed Schuyler of the Associated Press answering a
> question from a Japanese customs official on
> how long he expected to be working in Tokyo.

From the beginning of the telecast, Jim Lampley and Larry Merchant looked ill at ease. And ill at ease doesn't fit these two pros—knowledgeable, smooth, and confident maybe—but certainly not ill at ease. The boxing world was running out of challengers and venues. Relevancy of the sport was fading, and they, more than anyone else in sports, knew it. You could see it in their faces and hear it in their voices.

> *Lampley:* We are live inside Korakuen Stadium in To-
> kyo, Japan, as HBO Coors presents World Champi-
> onship Boxing. Tonight, undisputed heavyweight
> champion Mike Tyson casts the title defense against
> the challenger, James "Buster" Douglas. It is sched-
> uled for 12 rounds. A look around this soft ceiling,
> air-suspended dome, nicknamed "The Egg," is not
> unlike the Carrier Dome in Syracuse or the Silver
> Dome in Pontiac, Michigan. I'm Jim Lampley. We
> at HBO welcome you and the world to big-time box-
> ing. We are here in Japan to test the theory that ticket
> buyers on foreign shores will purchase what Ameri-
> cans seem increasingly unwilling to shell out for—
> apparent mismatches for Mike Tyson in defense of

59

his heavyweight crown. With me again is our HBO boxing expert, ring legend, Sugar Ray Leonard. Ray, we assume that it becomes increasingly difficult for Mike Tyson to prepare for boxing matches that most of us see as non-competitive. You spent a couple of hours with the champion two days ago; what was his mood?

Leonard: I'll tell you, Jim, it was a very interesting setting because, traditionally, Mike would have a number of people around him. But this particular time—this particular fight rather—he's had only a handful of people in his camp, the reason being, Mike Tyson is aware that he is always under the microscope, he's performing whether they go one round or 10 rounds. He's been highly criticized so he needs to be by himself in a more subdued and relaxed atmosphere, and that's where he is now.

Lampley: And of course, the man we like to have with us when we get ready to call one of these championship fights, HBO boxing analyst, the well-versed Larry Merchant. Larry, what are we about to see— another 90-second annihilation of an ill-prepared opponent?

Merchant: Well, in the important game of expectations, this fight is over before it begins or soon thereafter. You have to remember that just nobody believes anybody can compete with Mike Tyson. In fact, Ed Schuyler of the Associated Press when he arrived in Tokyo was asked by a customs official what he was doing here. He said he was here to cover the Tyson-Douglas fight. "How long do you expect to work?" the customs man asked. "Oh, about 90 seconds." The good news is Buster Douglas does have a history of fighting better against tougher opponents, so perhaps we'll get a few good rounds. Also, Douglas has a dog, a beagle named Shakespeare, and I believe that any prize fighter with a dog named Shakespeare can't be all bad.

Not exactly the words a fighter plans for his headstone, although points given to Merchant for clever and creative.

Lampley: Buster Douglas tells us that his favorite Shakespearian play is the romantic tragedy, *Romeo and Juliet.*

With those kinds of comments, one had the feeling HBO didn't travel to Tokyo for the money, but rather to hide out.

But it didn't look like Tyson came to Japan to hide. How is it possible that Mike Tyson would seem more at home and accepted in Tokyo, Japan, than in his own country? Is it simply that all people love a winner, especially a budding legend? Or *was* he Godzilla? Did the Japanese people see him as their old reptilian friend, stomping around their city, swaggering and mugging like he owned it?

And where was Buster? Well, according to his manager, Buster was taking care of business. This is the time in sports where fear can be your friend. One wouldn't suggest that Buster was afraid, and one wouldn't insult him by even asking the question. But many know enough about sports to understand what a great motivator fear can be, and that includes all forms of fear. There's a fine line between freezing up with fear and using fear as a motivator. Whatever the case, it was clear Buster was training the way a man who is on a mission—no matter the motivation—trains.

Lampley: Now we strain for a look at 29-year old Buster Douglas as he emerges from his dressing room where, we are told, he has spent most of the last hour resting quietly. His last fight, a 10-round decision over Oliver McCall, was on the undercard of Tyson's 93-second conquest of Carl "The Truth" Williams in Atlantic

City. You see on the TV screen his rankings: No. 2 for the IBF [International Boxing Federation], No. 3 for the WBC [World Boxing Council], and No. 4 for the WBA [World Boxing Association]. As a footnote, the No. 1–ranked heavyweight contender in all three governing bodies is Evander Holyfield who is here at ringside; and we expect to be talking live with him at the end of the bout.

Merchant: This is more animated than we usually see Buster Douglas so he is obviously excited. But now he has to go out and fight the most fearsome fighter on the planet. He will, however, go away with about a million dollars and that should cap his professional career quite nicely. If he gives a good performance, even if he doesn't win, he will be in line for more money. So he has a lot of motivation.

If comments like this don't demonstrate the quintessential definition of "underdog," I don't know what would.

Lampley: 34 official fights. He did have one bout which was ruled a no-contest. 19 knockouts among his 29 victories.

Merchant: And his two best victories were over fractional champions—champion for a few days, Greg Page and Trevor Berbick.

Lampley: [*Referring to TV screen graphics.*] Look at that weight progression. In his sixth pro fight back in 1981, he weighed 208. Two years later he weighed 260. He was over 240 last July when he fought Oliver McCall. Buster enters the ring tonight at 230 pounds, which would suggest that Buster is in pretty good shape.

Leonard: "This is a new Buster Douglas." That's what Buster told me.

Merchant: And here is a familiar Mike Tyson, rushing

toward the ring, wanting to get it on and get it over
with.

Lampley: Flanked by the entourage which, as Ray
Leonard pointed out, is dwindling in size from fight
to fight.

Merchant: Mike has termed this phase of a fight his favorite phase. He calls it like going out on a date—
it's finally going to happen. Of course his idea of a
date is wham, bam, thank you . . . sir.

Lampley: The man just inside of Tyson on screen, right
there, is Jay Bright, one of the two listed co-trainers.
Not in sight in this picture is Aaron Snowell, the other
co-trainer, they, of course, the men who inherited the
role of training Mike Tyson when Kevin Rooney was
expelled from camp. 37 wins, 33 knockouts, only
one decision in a title fight—and that was the 12-
rounder with Tony Tucker. Check that; there was also
a 12-round decision over "Bonecrusher" Smith in a
title fight.

Merchant: This picture right here is really one of the
more exciting moments in all of sports today. That's
watching this athlete [Tyson] waiting to get it on.
He's like a combination of a Pavarotti clearing his
throat and a bomb ready to go off.

Leonard: This is the worst part, waiting, 'cause you just
want to get the fight on. You don't want to wait around
for the ceremony, you just want to get up in the ring
and start the fight.

Lampley: Tyson has managed to completely ignore the
entreaties of Japanese officials in the ring who want
him to participate in a belt ceremony.

Merchant: He wants to do the belting right now.

Leonard: And it's always tough on the challenger because he has to wait.

Lampley: We're told that Mike was, as is often his custom, pounding the wall in his dressing room with his

fist in the half hour prior to his departure to come out to the ring. That was the case before his four-round knockout of Larry Holmes. It was the case before his 91-second destruction of Michael Spinks. A tale of the tape—you heard Mike Tyson say before the fight that he has always had a physical disadvantage against his opponents. And here it is again: height, weight, and reach all in Buster Douglas's favor. But Tyson, once again, is in great shape at 220.5 pounds. Let's listen to ring announcer Jimmy Lennon introduce the fighters.

Lennon: His record is 29 wins, four defeats, one draw, with 19 wins by way of knockout. He's ranked No. 3 by the WBC, No. 4 contender in the WBA, please welcome the challenger, James . . . "Buster" . . . Douglas! And his opponent, the defending champion on my left, needing no introduction the world over; he's ready to fight out of the red corner in the black trunks, hailing from the Catskills, New York, he weighed in at a ready 220.5 pounds. His outstanding record: 37 wins, no defeats, with 33 big wins by knockout. He's making a 10th defense of the heavyweight crown. Introducing the undefeated, undisputed heavyweight champion of the world, the one and only, "Iron" . . . Mike . . . Tyson!

ROUND ONE

That was a good round for Douglas. Probably the best round I've ever seen Buster Douglas fight, and I gave it to him.
—Larry Merchant

Tale Of The Tape

	Buster Douglas	Mike Tyson
Age	29	23
Height	6 feet 4 inches	5 feet 11 inches
Weight	237 pounds	220 pounds
Reach	83 inches	71 inches

After the prefight preliminaries in the ring, Referee Octavio Meyran finally announced, "Everybody out!" The three knock-down rule was in effect, and the fight was ready to begin.

❐ ❑ ❐

Larry Merchant: Douglas insists he's going to shock the world. If he should upset Tyson it would make the "shocks" of Eastern Europe seem like local ward politics.

Jim Lampley: He would shock most of the world if he could make it into the middle rounds.

Sugar Ray Leonard: He has to convince Mike Tyson the very first round.

Jim Lampley: Buster Douglas is a conventional fighter
  who likes to work behind a stiff left jab.

Mike Tyson, his eyes cold and staring into space, his face signaling dread, his chiseled body held taut like a spring set to uncoil violently after being wound beyond tight, paced the canvas like a watched panther in a cage. Dressed in bad-guy black trunks and rolled black socks that barely peeked out from his black, high-topped shoes, Tyson brought the same minimalist approach to his fashion as he did to his work in the ring. Minutes before the scheduled 12-round bout, he had entered the arena looking more the part of the street brawler he once had been rather than the undisputed heavyweight champion of the world that he had become. Instead of a tailored robe with "Iron Mike" or something similarly poetic and neon embroidered on the front and back, Tyson appeared during the ritual procession from the dressing room to the ring wearing a loose-fitting, sleeveless tunic that looked as if it had been cut from the remains of an old and battered bath towel. As was his routine, Tyson had spent the previous half hour pounding the walls in his dressing room. And as had been the case with most of his recent opponents, the walls had taken the punches while putting up little resistance.

Whether Tyson had any thoughts about possible resistance from James "Buster" Douglas, who, a few feet away from Tyson's pacing, danced while the red and white tassels on his white shoes flamboyantly shook and shimmied throughout his bouncing warm-up routine, the champ was keeping them to himself. If anything, Tyson publicly seemed to share the haughty consensus of the boxing world that in Douglas he had found yet another pigeon, easy prey. "No one, and I mean no one, will ever take my title away from me," he had proclaimed in the lead-up to the fight.

Douglas, who had a checkered ring past and at age 29 no longer deserved the designation as an up-and-comer, appeared to be no threat. In a rather thin heavyweight division, Douglas came in ranked as the No. 2 contender by the International Boxing Federation, No. 3 by the World Boxing Council, and No. 4 by the

World Boxing Association. While he had scored 19 knockouts in 34 fights, Douglas's 29-4-1 ring record was nothing more than that of a journeyman. True, he had beaten Greg Page and Trevor Berbick, but he had also lost to Jesse Ferguson and Mike White.

If Tyson seemed confident, even arrogant, the reasons were apparent. Since claiming the World Boxing Council championship on Nov. 22, 1986, by demolishing Trevor Berbick in two fierce rounds, Tyson had taken out each opponent—big name, little name, or no name. Sometimes he had done it without breaking a sweat. Tyson, himself only 23, had become the youngest undisputed heavyweight champion ever when he claimed the World Boxing Association belt—the final piece in unifying the title—with a unanimous decision over Tony Tucker on Aug.1, 1988. Since the start of his championship run, he had fought 10 title fights that had lasted a total of 52 rounds. No heavyweight— not Joe Frazier, not Joe Louis—took less time to dispose of challengers than Tyson's average of 5.2 rounds per title bout. Quick fights mean knockouts, and in that arena Tyson had put himself among the greats. 89 percent of Tyson's 37 professional bouts, all victories, had ended in knockouts. Only George Foreman, at 91 percent, had punched opponents into oblivion with more frequency.

Ring observers figured oblivion awaited Douglas in the Tokyo Dome on Feb. 11, 1990. So did most of the public. The betting odds had soared to 42-1 in Las Vegas, and the fight had been taken out of play by at least one casino because the one-sided betting had made the possible payoffs too risky. The bout itself was being held in Tokyo because nobody in the United States had been willing to come up with big money to witness another noncompetitive bout. If Carl Williams, Frank Bruno, Michael Spinks, and Tony Tubbs hadn't been able to earn their money with Tyson, what were the chances James Douglas would? "In the important game of expectations," said Larry Merchant, part of the HBO television broadcasting team, "this fight is over before it begins or shortly thereafter." Even though many Japanese considered Tyson a cult hero and the hosting of a world championship bout a matter of national pride, ticket sales had not been as robust as promoters hoped.

Only about 35,000 of the 63,000 seats at Korakuen Stadium would be filled, although all 3,000 seats near ringside had been scooped up at $1,000 apiece. In one of those grand seats sat Evander Holyfield, undefeated and the consensus No. 1 challenger to the title. Holyfield had been bypassed for a title shot this time, but his high noon was but a few months away. A fight with a $12 million payday for Holyfield had been set for June. Tyson merely had to finish today's business. Not only did the money for a Tyson-Holyfield match-up promise to make an oil sheik envious, it appeared to be only a round or two in Tokyo away from materializing.

As Tyson paced and Douglas danced, the talk among ring-side pundits was that Douglas had performed best against better opponents, and Tyson was indisputably Douglas's best opponent yet. So the possibility existed, a few experts suggested, that the challenger would last a few rounds. While nobody dared dispute, for fear of ridicule, who was the better fighter, there also was no question who was the bigger man. Douglas stood 6-4 to Tyson's 5-11. The challenger weighed a svelte, for him, 237 pounds to the champ's lean, muscular 220. At age 29, Douglas certainly was not past his physiological prime, while Tyson might be only on the threshold of his. Douglas had an enormous advantage in wing-span, 83 inches to Tyson's 71. Lack of reach, nonetheless, had yet to hurt the champion. Not only had Tyson gone unbeaten while routinely matched against bigger men, he had never been knocked down during a professional bout. Tyson's style was to duck punches, brawl his way inside and hammer at the body or the head with incredibly powerful punches. That attacking technique and its smashing results, particularly of late, created around Tyson an aura of invincibility. As a consequence, the champ already had grown accustomed to winning the mind game long before an opponent stepped into the ring.

This time, an air of uncertainty about the emotional state of each fighter coiled like thin smoke around both camps. Both fighters had cause to be distracted. Tyson recently had dismissed his longtime trainer Kevin Rooney and replaced him with Aaron Snowell, whose lack of experience in big fights raised questions about Tyson's judgment. As to his readiness, the champ had been knocked down in a sparring session by Greg Page. Some observers wanted to make something out of the knockdown other than the usual prebout hype.

Douglas, meanwhile, was approaching the fight of his life only weeks after he had lost his mother, Lula Pearl. Compounding the challenger's woes, only days before the bout the mother of his son had been diagnosed with a potentially life-threatening kidney condition. Douglas himself was getting over a respiratory ailment that only recently had left him weakened and made breathing difficult. The question of whether illness and turmoil could somehow lead to upset was about to be answered. Called together by referee Octavio Meyran, Tyson and Douglas stood face to glaring face shortly after noon, Tokyo time, to hear his instructions. As the ring was cleared and the boxers headed for their corners, Tyson looked again like the inescapable force, more myth than man. Based on that myth, Douglas had every reason to be wary, even frightened, of the damage Tyson could inflict with a single punch. To win, Douglas surely would have to box, but he would have to do more than just that. He would have to locate within himself some previously hidden power. He would have to exploit that power to fight the perfect fight. There really was no other way. Tyson, maybe only a man and not a myth, had proved himself the most devastating boxer of his era. The bell sounded. In less than an hour, questions would be answered. Hopes would be fulfilled or crushed.

From the opening bell it was obvious that Buster Douglas was moving well, his left jab crisp and accurate, Johnson's "stick" was working to perfection. He continued to impress into the first minute of the opening round.

Douglas did not move toward Tyson the way so many others lately had done, like a condemned man on the way to the gallows. Instead the big man floated; he glided; he bounced. And out of that mass of movement, Douglas flicked long left jabs that snapped at Tyson's uncharacteristically stationary head. If some suspected hubris had begun to creep into Tyson's game, here was the first evidence. The champ had not come to box, he had come to perfunctorily and brutally vanquish. Tyson had built a reputation, and, what's more, he apparently had come to believe in it. An unknown like Douglas, according to the storyline on which Tyson's aura rested, was meant to go down quickly. And so Tyson charged forward, absorbing and shrugging off Douglas's first tentative but accurate shots. He searched for the opening he felt would certainly appear as Buster's fear of being stalked overcame his ability to execute the fight plan devised John Johnson.

While Tyson's forward plodding showed disdain for Douglas's punching ability, the champ couldn't get close enough to do damage without taking some wicked shots, a situation Tyson seemed to accept. The champ appeared willing to absorb punches in order to work his way inside, the only position from which he, decidedly disadvantaged in reach, could launch his own weapons, including fearsome body shots. Douglas, jabbing with precision and dancing clear of the ropes, refused to let Tyson get close. Tyson resorted to a few lunging attempts at a stopping blow, but Douglas easily ducked and feinted or sidestepped the punches. Those early exchanges, which established the pattern for the fight, seemed invariably to favor Douglas. The challenger continually beat Tyson to the punch, often landing two blows before the champ could or would retaliate. The sparring made Tyson look lethargic, slow, unmotivated. However, whether Douglas actually was the quicker of the two can be debated.

The problem Tyson appeared unprepared to handle was Douglas's superior reach. As long as Douglas could keep moving on the periphery of his landing range, he could use that 12-inch reach advantage to unload shots against which Tyson could muster little tactical response, except to back off or try to close in. Tyson couldn't throw measured punches because he couldn't get near enough to land them. The lunging punches he resorted to, moreover, beg for the counter. Still, if Douglas was to make the fight more than a nice payday, he would have to continue what he had managed to do in the first round: punch from a long distance and stay out of Tyson's way. When Tyson did move inside, an inevitability unless he ran into an unlikely knockout punch, Douglas needed to continue avoiding the crippling body shots, as he did in the round, by wrapping up the champ until Meyran forced them to separate and reset.

Douglas demonstrated discipline, focus, and confidence, all three of which were important elements of Johnson's training plan. He showed no signs of anxiety or fear. By round's end, the challenger had piled up a surprising advantage in punches. Douglas had thrown 31 jabs and landed 12. Of Tyson's 13 jabs, only five had landed. At ringside, a stunned Larry Merchant declared that the round was, "probably the best round I've ever seen Buster Douglas fight," and belonged to the challenger. Tyson, who was looking for a knockout, probably wasn't counting jabs. At that point, neither was anyone else. "A number of fighters have had good first rounds against Tyson. Let's see if Douglas can sustain it," Merchant said.

Sugar Ray: I'm surprised to see Buster moving so well. I think the weight difference has helped. It is showing in the upper body and the legs. He's also doing a good job of tying Mike up every chance he gets.

Jim Lampley: Keep in mind that Carl Williams looked pretty loose and relaxed until Tyson hit him with a body punch almost 45 seconds into the first bout. Mike has not yet gone to the body against Douglas here.

Sugar Ray: Well, the left jab of Buster Douglas is incredible so far. Because he's one of the few guys I've seen other than Larry Holmes that can put a guy down with the left jab. So the left jab is the key weapon for Buster Douglas.

Jim Lampley: We're almost 90 seconds in and as yet Tyson has not done any real damage to Buster Douglas.

Meanwhile, Buster was connecting with great consistency,

especially with the left jab; Johnson's "stick" was working to perfection. Tyson already seemed confused and unable to respond. Early on it was Douglas, not Tyson, who looked in complete control.

Jim Lampley: Buster is punching on the break and gets a
>   warning from the referee.
>   Buster was coached by John Johnson to be the
>   aggressor. And so far he is being just that.
Jim Lampley: Watch that right hand of Douglas.

Thirty seconds later, again from Lampley, "A couple of more rights by Douglas!"

Sugar Ray: Tyson has to work extra hard to get inside
>   and that's Buster's advantage. [*:48 left in the round*]
Jim Lampley: Tyson has not yet gone to the body. Against
>   Frank Bruno, Tyson basically forgot Bruno's rib cage
>   for the first four rounds and paid a bit of a price for
>   it. Once he went to the body in round five, the fight
>   was over pretty quickly. [*:26 left in the round*]
Sugar Ray: See! Douglas is not allowing Mike to work
>   his body. He's trying to tie him up inside. In fact,
>   he's doing a pretty good job here. [*:10 left in round*]
Jim Lampley: [*Louder voice—excited*] Another right by
>   Douglas! And Tyson lands a left hook! [*:03 left in
>   round*]
Larry Merchant: That was a good round for Douglas and
>   I gave it to him!

12

ROUND TWO

*We talked about intimidation before the fight; Douglas has
so far shown no signs of intimidation.*

—Jim Lampley

The fact that Douglas had not only survived but apparently
won the first round raised questions among ringside observers at
the very outset of round two. Tyson seemed unusually docile,
Merchant told the HBO audience. Jim Lampley, who was calling
the fight, wondered whether Tyson was as sharp as he wanted to
be. The early returns, for what little they could be worth after
three minutes, favored the challenger. About 30 seconds into the
second round Tyson and Douglas exchanged a flurry of sharp
punches, and Douglas gave as much or more than he took. Before
a minute had elapsed, Douglas landed a head shot and partially
blocked a Tyson left hook during a second serious exchange. A
pattern that favored Douglas's long-range jabs and close clinches
continued to emerge. Tyson, who chose to brawl rather than to
box, was walking into scoring punches as he searched for a way
inside.

Tyson didn't yet realize it, but he was gambling with the
title. The champ was betting he could take Douglas's shots long
enough to find his knockout zone. The method had worked in
recent fights against opponents who panicked as Tyson walked
through their best punches. Douglas, however, appeared so intent
on carrying out the game plan created by Johnson that he had
dismissed the fear factor. Routinely, his mind apparently only on
his business, Douglas beat Tyson to the punch. With about one

73

minute left, Tyson broke through to land a hard body shot, his first of the fight. For the moment unfazed, Douglas answered a few seconds later with a solid right uppercut followed by several right/ left combinations that scored even if they didn't wobble the champ. The damage being done was being inflicted by the underdog.

By the round's end, Douglas had landed a fight total of 52 punches to Tyson's 16. Merchant declared the second round belonged to Douglas. Lampley agreed. The judges, as their cards would indicate eight rounds later, perhaps weren't as sure.

◻ ◻ ◻

Larry Merchant: That was a very docile round for Mike Tyson, throwing only 13 punches. But a number of fighters have had good first rounds. Let's see if Douglas can sustain it, Jim.

Jim Lampley: Let's keep in mind that Tyson, a little more than three weeks ago, was knocked down in training by Greg Page, and there was some talk here that he wasn't as sharp as he had been for previous bouts.

Sugar Ray: Every time that Mike comes inside, apparently Douglas has been doing a lot watching of films because he makes a move, he steps to his right, he gets a little angle.

Jim Lampley: Douglas giving as good as he gets inside right there! [*2:15 left in round*]

Larry Merchant: [*excited*] A very hard right hand by Douglas inside—and Tyson walked right into it! And right through it I might add.

Jim Lampley: We talked about intimidation before the fight. Douglas has so far shown no signs of intimidation. [*1:59 left in round*]

Sugar Ray: See, what they want from Tyson in the corner, they want to see more upper body movement, and also more punches thrown as opposed to the one big punch. And that's what Mike Tyson's doing now.

Jim Lampley: [*loud voice*] Another right hand lead lands for Douglas! [*1:24 left in round*]

Sugar Ray: Douglas is not afraid, that's apparent. What's happening Douglas is starting to get his punches off first, which is the key to boxing.

Jim Lampley: He's got pretty quick hands for a big man. [*1:13 left in round*]

Sugar Ray: Well, the lighter Douglas is, the faster his hands are, the more accurate his punches are.

Larry Merchant: [*loud voice*] Another good right hand and a good right uppercut, and two more good rights by Douglas! I don't think I've ever seen Tyson absorb that kind of a four or five-punch combination before in his professional career. [*:20 left in round*]

Sugar Ray: Mike is not attacking Buster Douglas, which indicates that there is respect here. [*:07 left in round*]

Larry Merchant: And also a little puzzlement Ray; he just doesn't seem to know how to go about it. [*bell rings*] That's another good round that I gave to Buster Douglas.

Jim Lampley: I don't think there's any doubt about that one.

Larry Merchant: Well, I don't know if he's gonna shock the world but Douglas has shocked me so far.

ROUND THREE

If Mike Tyson, who loves pigeons, was looking for a pigeon in this fight, he hasn't found him.

—Larry Merchant

As the third round began it was clear, even to a novice of the sport, how confident Buster Douglas was in the ring. He continued to move around the ring landing punches seemingly at will. Mike Tyson, on the other hand, looked confused, tentative, and not at all like a world champion. Although the experts at ringside were clearly stunned by what they were witnessing, one sensed they felt it was only a matter of time before Tyson unleashed the whirlwind.

During the break Tyson's corner man, Aaron Snowell, all but pleaded with his champion to work inside. Tyson responded as the round began by attempting a vicious, lunging right designed to make any need for tactical boxing irrelevant. However Douglas, wary of Tyson's impatience and quick trigger, slipped damage. The boxers then traded harmless punches, although Douglas continued to score points with his jabs, until a minute into the round Tyson unleashed a vicious body shot after Douglas had missed with a right hand to the head. Body shots, at least the way Tyson delivered them, would eventually take a toll on any opponent, but the short-term objective was to get Douglas to drop his hands. Dropped hands not only would open up Douglas's head as a potential landing site for cruise-missile punches but made flicking those quick, effective jabs more difficult. Douglas, though, would not drop his hands. Instead, seconds after the body shot,

Douglas landed a couple of short rights to the head. Tyson, unable to mount more than a one-punch counterattack, pressed inside and ran into two stinging left jabs.

Still, Tyson wasn't yet hurting enough and he'd had too much past success to rethink his attacking approach. He obviously respected Douglas's power but wasn't convinced the challenger could put him out. Tyson continued to fight flat-footed, holding his head stationary as he worked toward landing his own damaging shot. Douglas's jabs might not knock a strong-jawed fighter such as Tyson to the canvas, but cumulatively they could take a toll. Douglas still danced.

By the end of the round, which did not clearly belong to either boxer, Douglas had landed in three rounds the same number of punches, 73, as Tyson had thrown. Tyson had landed only 28. "You're not closing the gap, Mike. You've got to get inside," Snowell told his fighter.

❐ ❑ ❐

Jim Lampley: Good left jab to the body by Tyson. That's the kind of blow which [*sic*] has done a lot of damage to previous challengers.

Larry Merchant: Another good right, but Tyson comes right through it.

Jim Lampley: Douglas still is out landing Tyson, out throwing him.

Sugar Ray: Again, the Tyson corner is yelling to *work* his way in, not to walk in there, because that jeopardizes, puts you in a lot of trouble. [*2:15 left in round*]

Jim Lampley: Douglas, accurate with the jab. [*2:08 left in round*]

Sugar Ray: Now, what Douglas can't do—he can't allow himself to get frustrated and try to exchange with Tyson. That could be fatal. [*1:56 left in round*]

Sugar Ray: I'm surprised I don't see as many body shots thrown by Mike Tyson. That would bring those hands

James "Buster" Douglas, six years old.
Author's collection

Buster Douglas sparring with his father. *Author's collection*

John Johnson on the field with Ohio State football coach Woody Hayes at the 1976 Rose Bowl. *Author's collection*

Left to right, John Johnson, Larry Holmes, Woody Hayes, and Don King.
Author's collection

An out-of-shape Buster Douglas when he first started with John Johnson (right) and J. D. McCauley (left). *Author's collection*

In better shape and ready to take on the world.
Author's collection

John Johnson, Buster Douglas, and Buster's son Lamar before the fight in Tokyo.
Author's collection

J. D. McCauley (foreground) and John Johnson (background) rush into the ring to congratulate Buster Douglas. *Author's collection*

John Johnson and Buster Douglas at the "welcome home" press conference in Columbus, Ohio. *Author's collection*

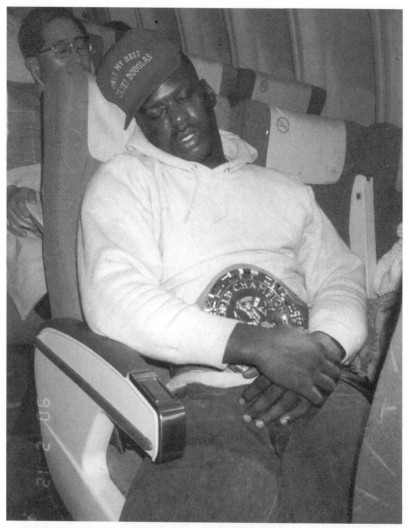

Buster Douglas gets some much-deserved rest on the flight home from
Tokyo. *Author's collection*

With the title win, John Johnson and Buster Douglas rubbed elbows with the rich and famous, including publishing giant John Johnson (center) . . .

. . . actor Gregory Peck (center) . . .

. . . Muhammad Ali (center) . . .

. . . and Julius Erving (far left) along with Vegas mogul Steve
Wynn (far right)

All photos from author's collection.

The undisputed heavyweight champion of the world.
Author's collection

down by Buster Douglas. [*1:43 left in round*]

Jim Lampley: Left and a right by Douglas. Tyson seems a little more precise in this round as he tries to move in. But it's still Douglas who is throwing and landing more often. Working behind the jab, as is his custom. Those right-hand leads have been very effective. [*1:22 left in round*]

Sugar Ray: They have been, but also you gotta get those hands back up. What Douglas is doing is he's not allowing Mike to get his punches to the mid-section. [*1:06 left in round*]

Jim Lampley: Douglas with another right hand to the top of Tyson's head. [*:29 left in round*]

Jim Lampley: Again, Tyson's corner yelling, "You've got to punch inside." [*:20 left*]

Jim Lampley: Good solid left jab by Douglas, Tyson grazed him with the right.[*bell rings*]

The experts at ringside were beginning to sense history in the making. And in Tyson's corner, things were beginning to unravel.

"You're not closing the gap, Mike."

"You gotta punch, Mike."

"Too flat-footed in there."

A close-up camera shot of Tyson reveals a man in a state of confusion. Tyson is confronted with a situation he's perhaps never experienced—an opponent more skilled and not intimidated, and a corner with no answers.

ROUND FOUR

*This is the first time since Kevin Rooney hasn't been with
Mike Tyson that he's needed some answers from the corner.
Let's see if he's got the right answers.*

—Larry Merchant

Tyson simply couldn't get inside. Douglas opened the round
with a series of left jabs against the planted and seemingly disen-
gaged champion. After the first few seconds the pace slowed,
which was not a particular surprise. Neither boxer had come into
the bout with a reputation for stamina; Tyson had been in few
long fights and the heavier Douglas had showed a tendency to
wear down in the past. Tyson was marking time as he looked for
the opening he was sure would materialize. Douglas, told by his
corner he had the lead in scoring, appeared to be willing to coast
for a while. The landscape quickly changed with about a minute
remaining. First, Douglas slammed Tyson with a long, jolting right
hand for which Tyson had no immediate answer. As the clock
wound down, Tyson delivered a crunching right to Douglas's head.
Rather than crumple, the challenger responded with a series of
combinations that left small margin for doubt about who was
sharper as the bell sounded.

Starting with the left jabs and ending with a flurry of solid
punches, Douglas seemed to have controlled yet another round.
Ringside statisticians had counted 114 jabs thrown by the challenger to that point in the fight. Worse yet for Tyson and his camp,
almost half of those jabs had landed. Snowell told Tyson he would
have to start moving his head. Douglas was beginning to leave marks.

❒ ❑ ❐

Larry Merchant: Tyson's corner is trying to make him just fight, not look to winging big punches, expecting Douglas to fall the first time he lands something.

Jim Lampley: And the man who does most of the talking in Tyson's corner, and he's leaning forward to whisper in his ear, Aaron Snowell.

Sugar Ray: If you watch what Douglas is doing now, he's trying to double that jab up, and see the second jab is not really hard, but it blinds you for a fraction of a second, that's when you drop the right hand. There was an expression on Tyson's face and I can relate to that, because sometimes you get into the ring, Jim, and you just don't have it. Things just don't click in. Maybe that's what he's feeling now. He's just not on.

Jim Lampley: Well gentleman, we're in round four and a lot of ringside observers didn't expect the fight to go this far. It should be pointed out that stamina has been a problem for Buster Douglas throughout his career, and in the last two weeks he's been bothered by a respiratory illness here. He's taken penicillin just this past week. You have to wonder how far he can go at this level of effectiveness. [*1:55 left in round*]

Jim Lampley: Douglas still landing the jab, and then steps away. Tyson seems less aggressive than is normally the case. Perhaps a little frustrated. [*1:25 left in round*]

Sugar Ray: Well, Buster Douglas is definitely inspired because of the tragedy of the passing of his mother. [*1:16 left in round*]

Jim Lampley: Everyone in Douglas's camp said that would be the case today. He was extremely close to his mother.

Jim Lampley: [*excited*] Right hand by Douglas . . . right on Tyson's chin! [*:57 left in round*]

Sugar Ray: The double jabs, especially with a big man, is difficult to penetrate, always difficult to penetrate. [*:50 left in round*]

Jim Lampley: Critics of Tyson say since the departure of Kevin Rooney he has been increasingly easy to hit. There's very little head movement here today. [*:40 left in round*]

Sugar Ray: I wouldn't necessarily agree with that. Mike Tyson is Mike Tyson; he's a natural fighter. Sometimes you just have to make a change. [*:29 left in round*]

Jim Lampley: You don't think that the loss of Rooney as a trainer has made any difference? [*:24 left in round*]

Sugar Ray: I don't really believe that. [*:20 left in round*]

Sugar Ray: Good left hook by Douglas! [*:06 left in round*]

Jim Lampley: Douglas again with a left and a right! And now Tyson lands a right hand and backs Buster up. But here comes Buster! [*bell rings*]

Larry Merchant: If Mike Tyson, who loves pigeons, was looking for a pigeon for this fight, he hasn't found him.

In Tyson's corner an air of desperation was evident. Manager Aaron Snowell was saying, "You got to use that seven to get inside, Mike, to back this guy up! And you got to move that head. All right? Get that rhythm!"

The opposite was the case in Douglas's corner as manager John Johnson began to smell an upset, telling Buster, "You've won all four rounds."

The TV camera captured a dapper and stunned Evander Holyfield at ringside. Merchant remarked, "And there, of course, is Evander Holyfield who has a guarantee of $12 million to fight Mike Tyson in June, and right now that $12 million is not in the bank."

15

ROUND FIVE

I think you have to say this is the most trouble Mike Tyson has ever been in at this stage of a title defense.

—Jim Lampley

Tyson proceeded to ignore his corner's advice. Early in the round Douglas continued to land snapping lefts, once followed by a stinging right to the head as Tyson plodded forward like a stoic soldier into the outer reaches of the enemy's field of fire. His shorter reach meant Tyson repeatedly had to enter a no-man's land in which he could be strafed by leading punches without getting close enough to detonate the bomb meant to decide the struggle. The unmoving head had become an easy target, and Douglas never let it escape his sights. Halfway through the round, Douglas took aim with a combination of solid head shots that not only seemed to shake Tyson but also exposed the champ's inability to return fire. Tyson's left eye, a bull's eye in Douglas's trajectory of right leads, clearly began to show swelling.

As the bell sounded, astonished observers were beginning to wake up to the dawning impossible. Tyson, matched against a nobody, was getting nowhere. The champ not only was failing to solve Douglas and getting hurt in the process, but he seemed unable or unwilling to heed the admonitions from his own corner to stop trying to be Iron Mike the Invincible and to start becoming Tyson the boxer. Buster Douglas had dominated another round, landing 33 punches to Tyson's 11. In the champ's corner, the concern in Snowell's voice was becoming apparent. An ice bag was pressed hard against Tyson's swelling eye.

❐ ❏ ❒

Jim Lampley: Trainer J. D. McCauley and manager John
Johnson very calm in the Douglas corner. He's thrown
114 jabs and has landed half of them; extremely effi-
cient behind the jab, Buster Douglas.

Larry Merchant: Word from the Douglas people tell Douglas he's won all four rounds and, shockingly, I agree.

Jim Lampley: Tyson lands a jab! This is the round in
which Tyson turned things around against Frank
Bruno. Right hand by Douglas lands again!

Sugar Ray: Douglas has been smart, very smart. He
throws his combinations then he ties him up.

Jim Lampley: There's just no head movement there, Ray.
Mike is a stationary target for this guy.

Sugar Ray: That's the reason his corner is petrified, because they see that Mike has become a target directly
in front of Buster Douglas.

Jim Lampley: Another right hand! Now Tyson seems to
be wobbly. Mike is not throwing back. Buster Douglas is completely dominating this round with jabs
and right crosses. [*1:36 left in round*]

Sugar Ray: What's going to do some damage now is if
Buster Douglas throws an uppercut. [*1:26 left in
round*]

Jim Lampley: Tyson leaps inside with a left hook. One
punch at a time though, that's all he's throwing. [*1:21
left in round*]

Sugar Ray: There's the uppercut!

Jim Lampley: Absolutely, the opening is there. [*1:10 left
in round*]

Sugar Ray: Buster Douglas is so relaxed. And this should
save him in the later rounds, if it should go that far.
[*1:05 left in round*]

Larry Merchant: It appears Ray, that Douglas is fighting
a master fight in the geometry of the fight. Every

time that Tyson appears ready to throw he just backs off a little bit and ruins his timing.

Sugar Ray: Thus far he's fought the perfect fight. Because he's not been a standing target, although he's not really running around.

Jim Lampley: There's a lot of swelling above Mike Tyson's left eye and it is partially closed. And that is from the right-hand leads that Buster Douglas has landed almost at will throughout the fight. [*:35 left in round*]

Jim Lampley: I think you have to say this is the most trouble Mike Tyson has ever been in at this stage of a title fight. [*:10 left in round*]

Larry Merchant: This is the most trouble, Jim, he's ever been in *any* stage of a title defense. [*:05 left in round*]

[*Bell*]

Larry Merchant: That's another round for Buster Douglas!

Jim Lampley: And he even dominated the exchange after the bell.

Larry Merchant: You remember the top of the show I said the good news is Buster Douglas only fights his best against the best opponents. This is even better news than that, from his point of view. And he has swelled up Tyson's eye and is dominating the fight right now.

[*Replay of the fifth is examined.*]

Larry Merchant: Now just watch the combinations. A long right, a jab-hook, and he has been doing this over and over. Every time Tyson takes a punch and wants to fire back, Douglas fires back before he can.

Jim Lampley: You begin to file through your memory for the biggest upset in heavyweight championship fight history.

Larry Merchant: I don't think there would be anything like this.

Jim Lampley: I agree.

Larry Merchant: This would create a new standard for upsets if this went on.

Jim Lampley: Clay and Braddock not as big as this.

16

ROUND SIX

Stay in control, this f—in' guy's scared to death.
—John Johnson

Douglas, advised by manager John Johnson and trainer J. D. McCauley, understood that while he was winning the fight and undoubtedly had hurt Tyson in the previous round, the champ remained explosively dangerous. Perhaps Tyson had never been in such serious trouble in the ring, certainly not in any of his championship bouts, but that was little reason for Douglas to abandon what had worked so spectacularly for five rounds. If Douglas was going to pull off the biggest upset in heavyweight history, he couldn't afford to stray from the program.

Considering, however, that the fight had already lasted far longer than almost anyone had anticipated, any plans Tyson may have had seemed in need of dramatic alteration. The champion, for the first time in the fight, appeared ready to go to work. In the opening minute of the round Tyson connected inside with two jarring right uppercuts, though Douglas's clinches made follow-up punches nearly impossible. As a result, Douglas remained unshaken and confident, while Tyson's eye, stung by an occasional jab, was closing. Tyson took to covering up, which proved an effective defense, to ward off Douglas's accurate head shots. Douglas did not press the action in the round, countering and for the most part slipping Tyson's punches, which came more frequently. Still, the champ couldn't get the challenger where he wanted all his opponents, backed against the ropes or in a corner from which there was no escape from his assaults.

Douglas floated in the middle of the ring, frustrating Tyson, who no longer could afford to take more battering to the closing eye and so was forced to abandon his straight-up stalking. Now resorting to actual boxing, Tyson, if not delivering the heavy-duty shots with which he had hoped to crush Douglas, was scoring points. At ringside, Merchant gave a round to Tyson for the first time in the fight. But the long view still decidedly favored Douglas, who had landed a total of 135 punches to Tyson's 56. At the halfway mark, the ringside assessment was shocking. Douglas appeared to have won every round but one.

❐ ❑ ❐

Larry Merchant: Question is the stamina of Douglas as you pointed out. Stamina has never been a problem for Mike Tyson's opponents in the past.

Sugar Ray: And I would question the stamina of Buster Douglas with this kind of pace, but again, he's *so* relaxed in there.

Jim Lampley: By the punchstat computation, in the fifth round Douglas out landed Tyson 3-1, 33 punches to 11. If anything his dominance is increasing.

Sugar Ray: Again, the lead-off right, I'm very surprised they're landing like they are. [*2:10 left in round*]

Jim Lampley: Tyson landed an uppercut inside. [*2:07 left in round*]

Larry Merchant: But the thing is he never gives Tyson a chance to use those amazing fast combinations. Even when he gets hit, it's one punch and he smothers him, or he fires back. [*1:42 left in round*]

Jim Lampley: Little more peek-a-boo defense from Tyson as he is clearly aware of the closing left eye. [*1:13 left in round*]

Sugar Ray: That becomes a factor, especially for the very first time. Experience plays a major role in that kind of handicap. [*1:08 left in round*]

Larry Merchant: One of the things that his great mentor, Cus D'Amato, use to tell him was, "it's no virtue to get hit, so keep your gloves up." [*1:00 left in round*]

Sugar Ray: What I don't see is the upper body movement from Tyson, and that's why Douglas is landing those kind of punches. [*:35 left in round*]

Sugar Ray: Lead-off right once again! Mike needs to pick the tempo of the fight up. He needs to make Douglas work. So far he has not done that. [*:19 left in round*]

Jim Lampley: Tyson missed with a leaping left. [*:01 left in round*] [*bell rings*] A confident Douglas goes back to his corner, well ahead on points you have to assume.

Total Punches Through Six Rounds

	Thrown	Landed
Tyson	132	56
Douglas	272	135

17

ROUND SEVEN

It was almost twenty-five years ago, when a 7 to 1 under-dog named Cassius Clay thoroughly frustrated and whipped a Sonny Liston in Miami Beach at a time when Liston was regarded as invincible. You have to go back that far to find something this shocking in a title fight.

—Jim Lampley

John Johnson in Douglas's corner said, "You got it won, just stay in control. This f—in' guy's scared to death."

Despite a swelling eye that eventually would make him a half-blind fighter, Tyson opened the round clearheaded and confident. After listening to his corner beg him to find himself, the champ was the first off his chair, meeting Douglas at center ring as if he wanted to prove that everything that had happened so far was fluke, fairy tale, a dream from which everyone, particularly Buster Douglas, would now be summarily awakened. However, Tyson still could not quite rouse his own mythical self. Increasingly bothered by the threat to his eye from Douglas's jabs and lead rights, the champ sleepwalked into drowsy caution as the round progressed. On the few occasions when Tyson managed to move inside past the challenger's long-range shots, his hardest punches failed to connect, landing on Douglas's arms or gloves, glancing off his cheek, or finding air instead of chin. At other times, Tyson simply could not uncoil punches because Douglas had him tied up.

Douglas also failed to mount much of an offense, resorting to reaction. The hardest blow he unleashed came about halfway through the round when he stung Tyson with a hard right to the head as the champ pressed forward. The round, full of sound and fury but little of consequence, appeared to be a physical standoff. All the while, though, Tyson's sun was being eclipsed on points. The jab count mounted in Douglas's favor, 89 landed to Tyson's 21, an indicator of dominance by the underdog. Though neither fighter appeared to be struggling to stay on his feet, Tyson was awakening to the realization his title might be in jeopardy. A point would come, if it had not already been reached, when only a knockout could save him. Only five rounds remained.

> *Jim Lampley:* Few at ringside thought that Buster Douglas would make it this far. He has made it this far with a dominant showing over Heavyweight Champion Mike Tyson.
>
> *Larry Merchant:* If this fight was being held in the States the crowd would be in an uproar right now.
>
> *Jim Lampley:* Here, they are eerily silent. Douglas continues to out land Tyson at close quarters and then tie him up. Douglas, with another right hand! Looping over the top. [*1:32 left in round*] Tyson's corner liked what it saw with the uppercut. [*:26 left in round*] It was almost 25 years ago, when a 7 to 1 underdog named Cassius Clay thoroughly frustrated and whipped a Sonny Liston in Miami Beach at a time when Liston was regarded as invincible. You have to go back that far to find something this shocking in a title fight.

18

ROUND EIGHT

We're in the eighth round, folks.

—Jim Lampley

In Tyson's corner, manager Aaron Snowell is fighting off a flashback. An overwhelming sensation is flooding over the experienced corner-man. Like a dream, he's suddenly back in Philadelphia, Pennsylvania, with the man who would change his life forever, Muhammad Ali. Throughout Aaron Snowell's life that first meeting with Ali never left him. From "dishes in the kitchen," as he calls his first job for Ali at age 12, to that historic corner with the world champion in Tokyo, the experience he received with Ali would get him through any tough situation. If John Johnson had Woody Hayes to see him through hard times, Snowell had Ali. All of his experience was telling Snowell it was this round or never. He knew his fighter was well behind Douglas in points and was in trouble. If Tyson didn't strike soon the heavyweight title would be history. He would have to figure out a way to make the champ focus.

Over in the opposite corner John Johnson couldn't help but think about Woody Hayes's favorite quote, from one of his favorite authors, Ralph Waldo Emerson, "Things are never as bad as they seem nor as good as they seem." Coach Hayes came up with the prophetic words after reading Emerson's Treatise, *Compensation.* As his fighter walked to the corner after dominating the seventh round (and every other round) Johnson's thoughts flooded back to his old mentor, ". . . things are never as good as they seem."

J. D. McCauley wasn't thinking about Ralph Waldo Emerson. J. D. McCauley was flying. McCauley thought he had been through it all in life by the time he arrived in Tokyo. But here he was in the corner with the next heavyweight champion of the world. He knew Buster perhaps better than anyone in the world and he knew, at that moment he just knew, it was his night. Buster was going to do it for all of them. But at the same time he couldn't help but have a rush of respect for the champion. Mike Tyson was taking a beating in the ring. For seven rounds Buster had pounded the champ . . . say what you want about the man, he wasn't going to lie down and hand his title to Buster. No, J. D. McCauley wasn't thinking about Emerson as he worked the corner in the eighth round, even as Woody Hayes's old voice whispered deep in his ear, ". . . things are never as good as they seem."

Averaging only 23 punches thrown each round, Tyson clearly had not come to Tokyo to demonstrate his sparring ability. His rationale of going for a knockout, and Douglas's thus far marvelous rebuttal, evidently was not leaving much room for doubt should a decision end up in the hands of the fight judges. As the deliberative outcome became apparently more in the challenger's favor with each unfolding round, Tyson came out swinging in the eighth, though he still was having serious landing problems. A minute in, Douglas, dancing again, got in a solid jab to Tyson's face. Douglas's jabs continued to land, and they increasingly hurt, especially whenever they worked Tyson's battered left eye. The exchange rate was picking up again and both fighters were sticking tactically with what had carried them through the first seven rounds. Noticeably more cautious now but nonetheless shrugging off the sting of Douglas's left jabs and lead rights, the one-eyed, single-minded Tyson kept struggling to step inside. Even when he did so successfully, his punches mostly misfired. After each wayward delivery by Tyson, Douglas held on, stepped back, or countered. If Tyson had reason to be frustrated, Douglas had cause to be confident. Tyson's increasingly sloppy ring habits, fostered by a string of easy victories and a subsequent growing lack of respect for opponents, were being exposed by a savvy fight plan and nerveless execution. Douglas was making what far more re-nowned fighters to date had found impossible look almost easy.

Competitors talk about being in the zone, an almost unat-tainable utopia where mind, body, and spirit coalesce harmoni-ously to create perfection. As far away from that zone as Tyson appeared to be, Douglas seemed to float in the middle of it. The bewildered champ, it was becoming improbably evident, appeared on this day less and less likely to touch the zoned-in Douglas. With 22 seconds left in the round, Douglas backed up a battered and beaten-looking Tyson with a looping right that might have put the champ down had it not glanced off his glove. Perhaps sensing a possibility he had not heretofore allowed himself to consider, for the first time in the fight Douglas followed inside with the intent to stay long enough to trade punches as Tyson retreated toward the ropes. The decision, which parted from the strict game plan laid down by Johnson and McCauley, quickly demonstrated why Douglas's corner didn't want its man to drift into ad-libbing. A missed Douglas right hand opened a small win-dow of vulnerability, and Tyson immediately crept through it with a hard right uppercut. Had the shot not caught the challenger with his head moving backward, resulting in little apparent damage, Douglas might never have had the chance to rethink his decision to trade blows inside Tyson's combat zone. Reminded by the er-rant punch to be cautious still, Douglas immediately chose to quickly tie up Tyson against the ropes before the champ could unload another bomb. When Meyan stepped in to separate the combatants, only seven seconds remained.

With Tyson against the ropes, Douglas at the break stayed to hang and spar until the bell rather than a retreat to the center of the ring. In the instant Douglas stepped back from the clinch and threw a perfunctory left job that glanced off Tyson's forehead, the champ uncoiled from a slight crouch with a tremendously quick and powerful uppercut that sneaked under Douglas's gloves and crashed like a full-force gale against the left side of the challenger's unprotected face. Out of some parallel universe inhabited only by athletic genius, that space that neither Douglas nor anyone else at ringside thought Tyson still occupied, the champ, with a single punch, appeared to have dismissed a hundred well-placed jabs, to have demolished months of carefully crafted plans, to have grounded soaring hopes. Tyson watched through one functioning eye as both of Douglas's eyes rolled upward. He saw Douglas's head move away in slow motion as it followed his toppling body down to the canvas. Douglas lay flat on his back staring into the white lights that burned in the inflated dome above. The end, in the way the experts and the touts had foreseen it, surely was at hand.

Yet, amazingly, either Douglas had not quite spent his luck or Tyson hadn't brought any. The champ had sent the challenger down with only seconds remaining in the round. Should Douglas get to his feet before Meyran could count to 10, the bell would sound, the round would end, and he would have a full minute to restore himself.

Meyran began his duty, his hand with fingers outstretched thrusting forward for emphasis as he repeated each ascending number. After almost five seconds on his back, a dazed Douglas rolled to his right, propped himself up on his elbow, slammed his left fist on the canvas and struggled like a newborn animal to rise on shaky legs. At six, Douglas rested for a moment on all fours. At eight, he pushed knees and elbows off the mat. At nine, a quavering Douglas stood upright. Meyran, peering hard into once-confident eyes for evidence of lucidity, nodded, looked toward Tyson's corner and brought the two fighters together to end what had started. Before Tyson and Douglas could more than glance at each other, the bell sounded. Douglas turned and as the stool came out walked to his corner, wobbling once like a thoroughly drunken man on his way to the bar. At the moment, nobody was counting punches anymore.

❏ ❑ ❐

Larry Merchant: Mike Tyson's anything but the dynamo, the dynamic terror that we're used to seeing. Buster Douglas has neutralized him, frustrated him, beating him to the punch.

Jim Lampley: Another solid, straight left jab right in the middle of Mike Tyson's face.

Jim Lampley: We're in the eight round folks. [*1:47 left in round*]

Jim Lampley: A heavyweight champion regarded as completely invincible in these circumstances is in big trouble. [*1:37 left in round*]

Jim Lampley: Did you ever imagine, Buster Douglas, undisputed heavyweight champion of the world? It boggles the mind.

Larry Merchant: Well, he's asking some questions of Tyson that Tyson hasn't been asked before. The second half of the fight, he's got to come back to win it. [*1:00 left in round*]

Jim Lampley: These right-hand leads are not diminishing in effectiveness, guys. He's landing just about all of them. [*:50 left in round*]

Sugar Ray: Double jabs, lead-off right hand.

Larry Merchant: Still beating Tyson to the punch. [*:28 left in round*] Well, there's just no question, which is the more competent fighter now. You see how easily Douglas is dominating the action inside. [*:23 left in round*] And Tyson is holding on. [*:16 left in round*]

Sugar Ray: I've never seen this happen before with Mike Tyson, he's always been the initiator. Here he's against the ropes.

Jim Lampley: And there's a right hand uppercut, and down goes Douglas! As suddenly as that.

Larry Merchant: Can he beat the count?

Jim Lampley: He got a little over confident, got a little loosey-goosey.

[*Bell rings*]

Jim Lampley: And the bell saves Buster Douglas in round eight.

Larry Merchant: Well, Tyson needed something like that and like a real champion he came through with it.

❏ ❏ ❏

Years later watching the fight, J. D. McCauley remembers, "We knew Buster was ready, didn't matter what everybody else was saying. But as much as I seen Buster fight since he was a little kid, I'd never seen him like he was that afternoon. I personally don't believe any fighter could've beat him that day. Maybe it was his mama in the ring with him. Whatever it was he couldn't be beat."

J. D. continues to watch the tape of the eighth round with pride.

"You know Buster and I are family. Look at him move in there. Don't no fighter his size move like Buster. Now watch him step off. Every time Tyson started toward him he takes a half step back, and that takes Tyson right off his game. See that little step right there, every time. He ate and slept that move, Buster sliding away from him, every time he get set to punch, slide to the right. Remember that John? It was well planned, slide to the right. It broke Tyson's rhythm all through the fight."

John Johnson remarks, "I don't remember seeing the punch that got Buster. Oh shit, there it is. Man, he did tag our boy. But I knew he was okay. I could see as he watched the count, Buster was not hurt."

McCauley continues, "I knew he was okay when he talked to us. The minute he opened his mouth in the corner, I knew. He said, 'I got him.' Isn't that what he said, John? 'I got him.'"

"People didn't realize what good shape Buster was in," Johnson insists. "I guess you can't blame them though, Buster was never more ready for a fight than he was in Tokyo."

McCauley picks it up from there. "I'll tell you another thing, nobody understood what good condition Tyson was in either. No fighter can take a beating from a man as strong as Buster for seven rounds and come back like Tyson, unless you're in great shape. That was one helluva punch that knocked Buster to the canvas."

Johnson agrees, saying, "That's true, J. D. It drove me crazy when I heard all those so-called experts after the fight say Tyson wasn't in shape for the fight. It was such bullshit. And not fair to Buster."

The look back has turned nostalgic. McCauley shakes his head and smiles. "Man, it seems like yesterday, watchin' this. They can never take that fight from us."

Once again, Johnson agrees. "Not your whole life can they take it away from us."

From Tyson's corner, Aaron Snowell reminisces. "I think Mike put everything that he had left into that punch." Snowell shakes his head as he watches the critical eighth round and the Douglas knockdown. "That was one shot. Great fighters can pull fights out in one shot and get out of a fight with a KO. Well, that was Mike's, 'get out of everything.' He pulled the trigger and it landed. He put so much into that shot. And the one great thing about Mike Tyson in Tokyo, it may've been the best fight he ever had because he never quit."

Snowell seems lost in thought as he projects to the end of the fight. "And you know all that talk about the messed up count? But that's what makes it a great event. Because it has all the mysterious, the, if this and if that, that's what makes a great sporting event, like the Steelers's pass. You know, the miracle catch for a game winning TD by Franco Harris, all the antics of great things. Certain things are decreed and you can't change it."

19

ROUND NINE

He's going to come like hell.

—John Johnson

For Tyson, the 60-second interlude between rounds seemed an eternity. For Douglas, it wasn't nearly long enough. The challenger needed more time to clear his head but, as the bell sounded, he knew what was coming. Tyson was going to attack. Douglas had to weather the onslaught until his head cleared. In the opening seconds, Tyson charged forward, leading with his left hand, but failed to inflict any real damage because Douglas ducked the punches or forced clinches. And each passing second of survival brought the scene into sharper focus for Douglas, until about 30 seconds into the round he surprised Tyson with a quick series of lefts and rights that signaled to the champ that the challenger was back in the fight. Awakened to the renewed peril by three solid shots to his head, Tyson responded only seconds later with a crushing right cross that wobbled Douglas again. However, the champ, arm-weary from throwing punches and punished into wariness by the cumulative effect of Douglas's eight-round barrage of pinpoint punches, could not find the resources to finish. Douglas, ducking yet another crisis, tied up Tyson. Nobody could know it, but Tyson had missed his last chance to knock out Douglas.

As the round progressed toward the final minute, both fighters, clearly fatigued, could muster only sporadically thrown long shots, few of which solidly landed, that typically ended in a clinch rather than a damaging combination. Out of a tie-up with 1:12 remaining, Douglas erupted with an explosive flurry of head shots that wobbled a suddenly retreating Tyson. As the champ leaned against the ropes to keep from going down, Douglas unloaded head and body punches until his strength gave out as the cornered Tyson somehow bobbed, blocked, and countered his way into one more clinch. Meyran stepped in with about 30 seconds to go, and both fighters stepped toward center ring. Despite weariness, Douglas was still firing. He caught Tyson with a series of rights and lefts to the head that again sent the champ backward against the ropes, but Tyson tied Douglas up, stalling the assault. After Meyran broke them apart, Douglas caught the immobile Tyson with a hard right to the head at 12 seconds. That, however, was the final damaging punch as the fighters fell into a clinch, and Meyran was unable to extricate them before the bell sounded.

As the fighters made their way to their respective corners, TV announcer Lampley described the ninth as "the most action-filled, heavy-punching exchange round of Mike Tyson's career." The ringside statisticians were counting again. Tyson, they said, had thrown 24 punches, landing 12, a 50-percent rate. Douglas, who at the end of eight appeared to be seconds from a knockout defeat, had come back in the ninth with a remarkable 58 punches thrown, 37—or 64 percent—of which had landed somewhere on Mike Tyson's body. The percentages appeared again to favor the challenger.

❒ ❒ ❒

Larry Merchant: Tyson is trying to find out immediately if his head is clear.
Sugar Ray: This is when Douglas should really do a great deal of clinching.
Jim Lampley: [*2:20 left in round*] Left hand lands by Tyson. He tries the uppercut again and misses. Douglas comes back with a left and a right! Three solid shots, right in Tyson's face! [*2:15 left in round*] There goes Tyson inside and up and under again. Solid right cross, Douglas wobbled again. Neither man playing much defense. At this moment they are just trading

shots, and now both men look a little weary.

Jim Lampley: Tyson misses with a right over the top. And Mike has slowed down, maybe a bit arm-weary. [*1:59 left in round*] This is high drama and the crowd here is greeting it, by and large, with stony silence. [*1:29 left in round*]

Larry Merchant: Probably disbelief, Jim. They came to see Godzilla and the wrong guy appears to be Godzilla.

Sugar Ray: The left eye of Mike Tyson is nearly closed now. [*1:16 left in round*]

Jim Lampley: Douglas coming back with a left and a right!

Larry Merchant: Tyson is hurt! [*1:10 left in round*]

Jim Lampley: Tyson is wobbling! Tyson needs the ropes for support, Douglas, wailing away. Without the ropes Tyson would've gone down. Plenty of time left in the round. [*:58 left in round*] Both fighters weary from the pitched battle. Mike Tyson was on the verge of going down. And again the champion wobbles back to the ropes! [*:24 left in round*] Solid right hand by Douglas!

[*Bell rings*]

Jim Lampley: The most action-filled, heavy-punching exchange round of Mike Tyson's boxing career!

Larry Merchant: And Mike Tyson is hurt, his eye is closing, and he is behind in this fight.

Sugar Ray: Just an incredible surge of strength and life in Buster Douglas.

Larry Merchant, looking at the replay, said, "Let's take a look. Two lefts and Buster Douglas is just going at him. And what he's doing is what other fighters who have had Tyson in trouble have backed off to admire their work, but when *he* got him in trouble he went at him."

20

ROUND TEN

Oh, the uppercut!

—Sugar Ray Leonard

Down goes Tyson! . . . Mike Tyson has been knocked out!

—Jim Lampley

Desperate, one-eyed, and only three rounds away from ig-
nominy, Tyson came out throwing. Unable to escape the likeli-
hood that he trailed in the fight and faced with the personal and
financial calamity that would come with defeat, Tyson caught
Douglas with a jolting right in the opening seconds. But the punch,
whether diminished by his own fatigue and awakening despair or
dismissed by the determined and revived confidence of Buster
Douglas, had no effect except to allay momentarily the sense of
doom that crept out of Tyson's corner and that cast a shroud of
disbelieving silence on the Japanese crowd. A minute drained from
the clock, another minute that belonged to Douglas. And at last
Tyson's frustrated fury was leading to wanton recklessness. The
champ now seemed eager to absorb Douglas's jabs and right leads
for a chance to end the fight with the punch that had disposed of
Williams, Bruno, Spinks, Tubbs, Holmes, Biggs, and 26 others
who had fallen by knockout.

Still searching for that silencer, the half-blind Tyson wan-
dered into three left jabs that forced him to cover his head and
drop into a crouch. For a moment, he could not see Douglas. As
Tyson attempted to peer over the top of his gloves, Douglas stuck
yet another jab aimed at the swollen left eye as, simultaneously,

107

Tyson, still trying to move forward, spread his gloves apart. Douglas instinctively shot in a straight left. The weak jab did no damage, but Douglas's glove covered Tyson's right eye. The champ was at that instant blind. And at that instant, as the champ, his gloves askew, fought blind and defenseless, Douglas was starting to bring a fully loaded right hand from the area of his waist. The right landed with 1:54 left in the round, crashing into the right side of Tyson's jaw from below. In the next stripped-down instant, Tyson's head snapped upward as a halo of sweat, shaken loose from his wincing face by the explosive thrust of the punch, shone in the ring lights, and immediately vanished like an evaporating crown. As a spray of salty water rained through the air, Tyson, carried by his own desperate momentum, began to fall forward. Douglas pushed the heavy body away, then chased it to the canvas with four symmetrical crossing blows to the head—two rights and two lefts.

With 1:52 left in the round, as the back of Tyson's head slammed against the canvas, his mouthpiece erupted from his lips and bounced to rest a foot from his upturned face and within reach of his outstretched arms. Tyson did not hit the ropes as he fell, but his head rested under them as he went sliding into Douglas's corner. When Tyson opened his eyes a moment after the fall, the first thing he saw was the red, white, and blues ropes that surrounded the ring. The next thing he saw was Meyran, who crouched over the champion and began the count at 1:49, just as Tyson was raising his head from the mat. At the count of two, Tyson rolled slightly to the right, enough to prop up his upper body on his elbow. At four, he completed the roll and rested on all fours and stared at the canvas. At seven, Tyson was up on his hands. Spotting the mouthpiece, he grabbed it and made a clumsy attempt to place it in his mouth. He only partially succeeded, and the white rubber piece dangled from his lips like the swollen tongue of a dead animal. One second later, Tyson rose to one knee. He wobbled backward and then to his side as Meyran counted. Meyran shouted 10 and waved his arms. The fight was over. A second later, Tyson stood on his feet, and Meyran wrapped his arms around the now-former champion as a signal to stop.

"Unbelievable," said Sugar Ray Leonard, the one-time welterweight title-holder, speaking for every witness to the act deemed impossible either by expertise or common sense.

Douglas threw his arms in the air. Johnson and McCauley hugged—each other, Douglas, whoever got within range. The ring rolled like a stormy ocean as bodies propelled by jubilation jumped wildly up and down.

❑ ❑ ❑

Jim Lampley: Oh, what a right hand by Tyson to lead off the 10th round! Larry, this has been an inspired, courageous performance by a man whose mother has died within the last month. Whose son's mother is battling a difficult kidney ailment, who had every reason to come into this bout depressed and downtrodden, chosen by no one to have a chance of getting out of the first few rounds, and yet he's thoroughly dominating Mike Tyson with exception of the moment when he went down.

Sugar Ray: Well, the other day John Johnson, Douglas's manager, said, and Douglas himself said, "I am a new person." Apparently he is.

Jim Lampley: It's been a whole different person than the one every boxing expert expected to see here.

Larry Merchant: It appears that Tyson is virtually a one-eyed fighter at this point. [*2:04 left in round*]

Jim Lampley: A desperate one-eyed fighter. [*2:00 left in round*]

Sugar Ray: Oh, the uppercut! [*1:54 left in round*]

Jim Lampley: What an uppercut by Douglas . . . and down goes Tyson!

Sugar Ray: It's over!

Larry Merchant: It's over!

Jim Lampley: Mike Tyson's been counted out!

Sugar Ray: Unbelievable.

Larry Merchant: This makes Cinderella look like a sad

story, what Buster Douglas has done here tonight.

Jim Lampley: Let's go ahead and call it . . . the biggest upset in the history of heavyweight championship fights! Say it now gentleman, James "Buster" Douglas, undisputed heavyweight champion of the world.

Larry Merchant: I would be willing to say it's the greatest upset in boxing history.

Larry Merchant: In Las Vegas they wouldn't even put up any odds on the fight—and suddenly Mike Tyson, perceived as the giant monolith, has been reduced to being just another champion who got defeated.

Jim Lampley: And you heard Aaron Snowell saying to Tyson, who apparently was unaware, "you were counted out. KO." The victory for Buster Douglas couldn't have been more richly deserved.

Sugar Ray: Well, Douglas did what a few guys have done in the past who've hurt Tyson, and didn't take advantage of it. Buster, inspired by the death of his mother, came on very strong. He had Tyson in trouble a few times. The uppercut—that pretty much was the bread and butter for the fight. It wasn't just the power of the punches but the accuracy and the number of punches that Buster Douglas threw.

Jim Lampley: Sustained accuracy all through the bout, for 10 straight rounds he was sharper and crisper and more accurate than the champion. If it weren't so improbable to believe that Buster Douglas would knock out Mike Tyson, you might've begun to say in the middle rounds that it was inevitable, as Tyson's eye closed and as he began to wobble in the inside exchanges. But, nevertheless, given the history of the champion you continued to wait and wait for the moment when he would, with sudden fierceness, be able to turn things around. And he did knock Douglas down with an uppercut at the end of Round 8. But Douglas came back to out-class Tyson in face-to-face exchanges throughout Round 9. And in the 10th he took over once again and finished Tyson with the combination you saw.

Sugar Ray: That was the turning point, Jim, when he was knocked down in the eighth and came back strong in the ninth round.

Jim Lampley: A heart as big as Japan's economic power.

If reserved described the reaction of the Japanese crowd, then bedlam could only describe what was happening in the Douglas corner. Johnson talks about the final two rounds.

"When James came back to the corner and sat down after the eighth round no one in our corner asked him if he was hurt. We knew he was in good shape. The first thing I said to him was, 'He's going to come like hell. Do you understand? He's going to come like hell!' Because I knew exactly what Tyson was going to do. At the bell he would be coming hard to our corner for the kill; I told James, 'stay down and throw straight.'

"The bell rang and as I predicted Tyson came winging in with a big overhand right, and he caught James. But James came right back and just started pummeling Tyson, completely dominating him, pinned him on the ropes and just punished him.

"Tim May of the *Columbus Dispatch* said it was one of the great rounds in all of boxing history. Of course, I think it was one of the great *fights* in heavyweight history. I watched Tyson walk back to his corner, he was staggering."

The tenth round, of course, created history. Some say it was the greatest upset in boxing, maybe all sports, history. *Ring Magazine* called it "the upset of the century." Johnson reflects back to the round, "At the bell James made a little move with his feet, and jumped to the side, and caught Tyson with a deadly uppercut. He followed with a right to Tyson's cheek and as he started down James finished him off with a stick. Tyson landed right in front of our corner. As soon as he hit the canvas I leaped up, I cupped my hands together and started yelling as loud as I could, 'Stay down! Stay down!' I was so insane at that moment I remember thinking that by screaming at Tyson maybe I could get in his mind and help keep him down; crazy, huh? There's a picture of me going into the ring at the ten count. I'm flying through the air trying to get to James.

"When the referee's count hit seven," Johnson continued, "Mike rolled over to get his mouthpiece and I knew then we had won. I got ready to get in the ring . . . J. D. actually beat me to James and we sort of collided. I then started to hug James, repeating over and over 'You were great! You were great!' Everyone in the corner was great that afternoon in Tokyo."

The ring announcer made it official. "Ladies and gentlemen, 1 minute and 23 seconds into round number 10, the winner by way of knockout, and new heavyweight champion of the world, James 'Buster' Douglas!"

❏ ❑ ❐

Jim Lampley: Larry Merchant is with the new champion at ringside. Larry, if you can hear me, take it away— it's all yours.

Larry Merchant: All right, I'm with Buster Douglas. Buster Douglas, undisputed heavyweight champion of the world—can you believe it?

Buster Douglas: Yeah.

Larry Merchant: Why did it happen, James?

Buster Douglas: 'Cause I wanted it.

Larry Merchant: Why, why did you win this fight that nobody on this planet gave you a chance to win?

Buster Douglas: For my mother, my mother; god bless her heart.

Larry Merchant: Are you saying you came out here more animated than we've ever seen you, more focused than we've ever seen you; and you're crediting it to the fact that the death of your mother? Just what focused your mind?

Buster Douglas: It was already focused.

Larry Merchant: What surprised you from the get-go?

Buster Douglas: Just what I did. Whup his ass. He come [*sic*] to fight; I come to fight. I told you in that room, I said it was time for James D. to come out of the closet. You know, I told you that I also had times when I had great fights. But then I'd come back with two or three little fights when I was mediocre. And I would leave a lot of doubt. I don't blame you guys; you guys are going with what you see, you understand? But I know, and my people know, that this is what the real James Douglas is all about.

Larry Merchant: Every challenger for Mike Tyson says the same thing, but you did something there to neutralize him . . . OK, just one moment, Buster."

Buster Douglas: I told you in the room, those other guys weren't James Douglas.

Larry Merchant: But you didn't let him get off. It seemed that every time he wanted to throw a punch you either beat him to it or you smothered him. Was that the idea?

Buster Douglas: I did what I did. I went out there and fought my fight. Very tough, very focused.

Larry Merchant: I know you had him, but you got knocked down.

Buster Douglas: Well, yeah, that was a good shot. Like I said before, a man over 200 pounds has a good shot.

Larry Merchant: Did you get careless? Did you think?

Buster Douglas: I think so. I was just starting to get real relaxed, and I got hooked. And I came back and sucked it up, 'cause I knew I still had him, I knew every time he tried to get off, I would come back and offset him by beating him to the punch. Early in the fight Mike would come out and throw his big shots, so what I would do is just go them with and come back with my own. Another thing, I was very relaxed;

I wasn't afraid of the man. I fear no man because I believe in God—that's the only man I fear. Thank god and praise the lord Jesus Christ.

Larry Merchant: But you know that you're in there with Tyson. After the knockdown, did you think that he would come on, or did you know you had to stop his momentum at that point?

Buster Douglas: Well, yes, I know he was going to come 'cause he's the champion. He's going to suck it up and come and get me. And I was ready for it; I was aware of everything, I was totally aware of everything. And dad, this one's for you. I love you!

Larry Merchant: Did you see the confusion in his eyes? Of course, one of his eyes was closed.

Buster Douglas: Well, I seen [*sic*] that early on because of my stiff jab; I have tremendous speed. I have tremendous ability. As I told you earlier in the room, I'm conditioned to go 12 rounds; that's what I'm conditioned for. And that is why I was able to get up from the knockdown. You know it was a good shot and I give him all the respect for that. But when I got up, it was like, well, it's time to go ahead and get him out of there.

Larry Merchant: You hit him with . . .

Buster Douglas: I got careless, I got careless, man. And then all of a sudden he caught me with a good shot.

Larry Merchant: You took some fearsome, he took some fearsome punches.

[*The crowd moves closer to Douglas and Merchant. Douglas's handlers surround, him disrupting the interview, and place the championship belt on Buster.*]

Buster Douglas: [*reacting to the championship belt*] It's a dream! I swear to god, it's a dream! This is truly a dream. I watched you all on HBO from time to time putting belts on guys and interviewing guys and I said one day it's gonna be me, one day it's gonna be me. And thank god, it was me today.

Larry Merchant: You hit him with some fearsome punches early, and he didn't seem to weaken.

Buster Douglas: Well, that's great because, you understand, like my dad said, you hit him with a shot, let him take it, let him be a tough guy. You just keep chopping on him and chopping on him and eventually he's gonna [*sic*] go. And that's what happened as you seen [*sic*] over there: he was flat on his ass.

Larry Merchant: I think that tells the whole story: Mike Tyson flat on his whatever you want to call it.

Jim Lampley: James "Buster" Douglas, 29 years old from Columbus, Ohio, undisputed heavyweight champion of the world. Well, if you're a sports fan, you know you've seen it a dozen times. How many times has a story so sentimental, so poignant, so emotionally powerful seemed to simply take over reality and tell itself? Surely, the sentimentalist in all of us wanted to believe that, in the wake of the death of his mother and amidst the difficulty being suffered by the mother of his child, James "Buster" Douglas could step forth today with a performance unlike any other in his career and compete with Mike Tyson. Surely the realists in all of said no, that wasn't really possible. But indeed, it was possible; and it happened. And an inspired Buster Douglas thoroughly dominated Mike Tyson and courageously came back from an eighth-round knockdown to turn around and knock the champion out himself. Larry Merchant, it has to be one of the greatest and most memorable moments in the history of the sport.

Larry Merchant: Well, it certainly is. I wish it had been in the United States after all, but Buster Douglas is an athlete. He played football and basketball in high school. He had a scholarship as a power forward to his junior college. He had ability. And I was very moved by the way he said he did it also for his dad. His dad was a terrific, spirited fighter—middleweight and light heavyweight—and was never satisfied with his son who seems to be so casual about it all. But for whatever human reasons possible, for someone to surpass his own abilities, to surpass anything that he could ever do before in this moment—at this moment—that's what makes this sport so terrific.

Jim Lampley: Incidentally, you're probably wondering if we are going to hear from Mike Tyson. We sent our Sugar Ray Leonard to follow Tyson to his dressing room to seek an interview with the former heavyweight champion, and Ray has been turned down. So, apparently, Mike will have nothing to say to us on this live telecast about his devastating 10th-round knockout defeat today at the hands of the new undisputed heavyweight champion of the world, James "Buster" Douglas—the fight that I have already called the biggest upset in the history of heavyweight championship boxing history and which Larry has gone me one better by calling it the biggest upset in boxing history.

Larry Merchant: You know, I'm just reminded that I've gone to the Tokyo fish market. This is one of the greatest spectacles on earth. As far as you can see there's huge frozen tuna because the Japanese love tuna so much. When I was standing there looking at it, I thought, well, Buster Douglas is just another frozen tuna. The guy just doesn't have it; we've never seen him with this much life, this much animation, or determination. But boxing is the theater of the unexpected; and when you least expect it, we had the unexpected.

Jim Lampley: Speaking of the unexpected, and why you never take anything for granted in a prizefight, Larry, look at these judges' scores. To the point in the bout at which Douglas knocked Tyson out, one judge, the United States judge, had Buster Douglas leading 88 to 82. But look at this: one Japanese judge had Tyson leading 87 to 86. It's hard for us to image what fight he was watching. The other Japanese judge had the fight even, 86-86. So if it had continued that way through the last two rounds, there was at least a chance of a draw or even a decision in favor of Mike Tyson which I think we both would agree would have been thoroughly unjust.

Larry Merchant: And the biggest injustice in boxing if that had happened. I just think that, judging from the reaction of the crowd is that they just couldn't believe what they were seeing. The Japanese basically came out to see Michael Jackson, Madonna, or The Rolling Stones—they came out to see a great performer be a star on the world's stage. And they just couldn't get their minds clicked into what they were seeing. That's why I said earlier in the fight, before the show, the importance of expectations in a fight and how that shapes what you're watching. Sometimes it takes a long time to believe what you're actually seeing in a prizefight.

Jim Lampley: In case you've just joined us, you missed a shocker. The once undefeated and undisputed heavyweight champion of the world, Mike Tyson, is no more. He's 37 and one now instead of 38 and zero. He was knocked out 1 minute and 23 seconds into the 10th round by a journeyman named James "Buster" Douglas who, now at age 29, a few weeks after the death of his mother and in the wake of learning about a life-threatening illness of the mother of his child, came up with the most inspired performance of his boxing career and is now the undisputed heavyweight champion of the world.

❏ ❏ ❏

Larry Merchant reflects back on the fight, the result, and where it stands in his 30 years of calling boxing matches.

"Among the things I remember most about those unforgettable days and nights in Japan was John Johnson's never-wavering belief and confidence in Buster Douglas. Looking back I believe the combination of the death of Buster's mother just weeks before the fight and John Johnson's guiding persona were the main contributors to Buster's success against Tyson." Merchant chuckles to himself as thinks back. "I remember asking Johnson just before the fight how Buster was going to beat the seemingly unbeatable Tyson. Without hesitation Johnson, smiling, says, 'He's going to hit him and then he's going to hit him again.'"

Merchant continued, "I attended a dinner the night before the fight where Don King, Donald Trump, and Shelly Finkel [Evander Holyfield's manager] were huddling, planning for the 'real' fight, the upcoming battle between Holyfield and Tyson. As I listened to the three of them make plans for their $20-million bonanza it became piercingly clear these guys didn't consider Buster Douglas anything more than a warm-up for the main event. Sitting there I couldn't help but think of the old boxing maxim that goes something like this: 'If you don't take your opponent seriously you turn him into a serious opponent.' Due to the unique individual nature of boxing, more than any other sport, it's deadly to take your opponent for granted."

When asked how he compared the Tyson-Douglas fight to all the bouts he's witnessed, Merchant relates, "I've called over a thousand fights in my career and I was never more shocked at a result than I was that day in Tokyo." He continues, "But in hindsight all the elements were there. Buster was a great athlete, he had the reach and the quickness, he had the motivation and the right guidance, his opponent was over-confident, and most important of all he had the right DNA."

Buster hit him, and then he hit him again. And walked away the world heavyweight champion.

21

CONTROVERSY

The first knockout obliterated the second knockout, Tyson won.

—Don King

W hat happened immediately after this magnificent fight can only be described as a disgrace. Perhaps what transpired is the perfect metaphor of the sport itself. And in the end the new world champion missed the opportunity of a lifetime, an opportunity that, it has to be said, diminishes the world title that he fought so gallantly to achieve.

The exact nature of the disgrace belongs to the exclusive confines of boxing. It all begins with the fact that, uniquely in this sport, a person can be the promoter of both fighters in the same bout. There hasn't been a monopoly like this since Standard Oil. Of course, we're referring to Don King. Just for the record, it should be noted that for this heavyweight championship fight King was the promoter of the fight and represented *both* Tyson and Douglas. I guess one can't blame King, after all, this is America, and in America it's all about making the money— even in Japan. Can't think of a better way of making money than owning both sides of a bet, and that's essentially what this is, isn't it? So, how can this happen? The best answer available, "Well, it's just boxing." But that's not good enough. We all know it's just a sport, just entertainment after all, and not oil. But one doesn't have to be a sports expert to know that boxing is in a reputation quagmire. Perhaps a first step out of the mess would be to address this very situation. No form of logic can persuade one to accept this promotions arrangement. And if you're not convinced yet, then what transpired after the Tokyo fight might help move you in a different direction.

Even though King technically represented Douglas, he needed Tyson to win this fight. And more importantly in the authors' judgment, he expected Tyson to win. You see, King had already signed Tyson and Evander Holyfield to fight for the championship after Tyson was to have put away Douglas in Tokyo. He signed them *before* the fight, just a little match for 20 million dollars. Buster, of course, royally screwed things up by flooring Tyson in the 10th round. That's why it was a squirming, hair-hat of a Don King sitting at ringside in Tokyo. So how does King remedy his 20-million-dollar problem? He contests the outcome of the fight. He tries to keep the title belt away from the very man he represents. Maybe King thinks he's the Monty Python of boxing promotion. You know, you represent Buster Douglas, but you really, *really* represent Mike Tyson. It's difficult to imagine any other enterprise on the planet, whether sports, entertainment, or corporate, that would legally or morally stand for such openly corrupt behavior. To put this in proper perspective, at the trial that followed this valiant effort by Douglas, Don King would testify under oath the following: "Buster is a boring, lazy fighter. He is the kind of fighter people throw hot dogs and beer cans at. When Buster fights everybody went [sic] out to buy hotdogs. Nobody wanted to see Buster fight. I moved him up in the rankings through attrition, without him having to fight anybody . . . I had to take Buster to Japan because I couldn't sell him in America." It became quickly clear to John Johnson that Don King did not attend Woody Hayes's school of loyalty.

Within an hour after Buster Douglas heroically achieved his lifelong ambition, the undisputed heavyweight championship of the world, Don King was frantically busy attempting to take it away. Shamefully, he cornered officials from the WBC and WBA in a private room and browbeat them into withholding recognition of the new champion. King then went on the public relations offensive. He immediately made the case that the count in the eighth-round knockdown of Douglas was flawed. King concluded that the referee had missed four seconds when he picked up the count from the timekeeper. But King had to know that the time-keeper is irrelevant. Douglas's only responsibility was to watch the count of the referee, which is exactly what he did. Indeed there was a discrepancy, but it has no official meaning, and everybody associated with the sport of boxing knows it. It didn't stop Don King. "Here's the facts [*sic*]," King would publicly announce almost immediately after the fight (King's comments were recorded by sports writer Sam Donnellon). "Mike Tyson knocked out Buster Douglas. Douglas was knocked out and the referee did not do his job. If the rule is kept, the first knockout automatically obliterates the second one; the man knocked the man out officially in the ring. The count went to 13. I issued a protest to Mr. Mendoza and Mr. Sulaiman. . . . It's a grave injustice here, it's a grave injustice if the decision holds that Mike Tyson was knocked out. The fact is Buster Douglas got knocked out first, and I expect them to do justice, that's what they're here for. The first knockout obliterated the second knockout, Tyson won." Keep in mind Don King represented Buster Douglas.

King was just beginning. Next, Don King continued his domineering pressure against the WBC and WBA officials insisting that they declare Mike Tyson the actual winner of the fight. King worked his arm-twisting magic behind closed doors against Jose Sulaiman, president of the WBC and Gilberto Mendoza, president of the WBC. The result—Sulaiman finally publicly announced: "I am suspending the recognition of *anybody* as champion." Mendoza agreed, coup de grace complete. Sulaiman continued the debacle by stating that the final decision on who won the fight would be made at a WBC meeting in 10 days. Anyone close to the sport at the time knew what this meant: the stripping of the world title from Buster Douglas.

What followed was the quintessential example of the importance of a free press, and ultimately the power of the media. The broadcast media covering the fight and its aftermath were unrelenting in the protest of Don King's attempted mugging. But they would be considered calm compared to the print media that followed.

Mike Lupica from the *National* wrote:

So it figures that the first reaction to Buster Douglas would be for Don King and Mike Tyson, and the WBC and the WBA, to think about stealing the night. They can't help themselves. These are people you wouldn't trust around silverware.

Douglas beat up Tyson and finally knocked him out. No one knows better than Tyson. Still Tyson tries to steal the night. Maybe he is nothing more than a common thug after all. Maybe he should look out, because whatever Don King has you can catch.

If the WBC and the WBA take away the title the world saw Buster Douglas win, if they take that night and try to leave it in a junk heap, then King has bought them.

Don King has become such a complete slob as a promoter he cannot see how bad Tyson looks trying to win a fight in a hearing room or a courtroom, when he didn't have the game to win it in the ring.

King and Tyson, true to their instincts, immediately look to take the other fighter's wallet.

Pete Dexter writing for the *San Jose Mercury News* put it this way:

Sitting at the same table, of course, is one Don King, who owns promotional rights to Tyson for the next 100 years, and probably the rights to all his children.

For 15 cents King will put his boys in the ring, and the girls on the streets. He is the easiest to imagine as a disease.

Mike Tyson, beaten up and knocked out in the ring, sitting in sunglasses, complaining he lost on a technicality. One by one he has sold out his friends for Don King— sold out even the memory of Jimmy Jacobs, who loved him and took care of him a long time before Tyson was worth anything—and now he has sold himself. Sold the last integrity he had left—his physical integrity—for Don King.

And that is how for a short time this week—until the world-wide public censure finally finds its way even into the dark holes where the governing bodies of boxing do business, and Don King is prompted to say his attempt to overturn what happened in the ring was "misinterpreted"— the greatest warrior of our time is transformed into a crybaby. The disease is Don King and Mike Tyson rots in front of our eyes.

And Joe Gergen in *Newsday* had this to say:

The man [Tyson] declined to discuss the bout immediately afterward, and when he did appear at a news conference a few hours later, he mouthed the King party line: "I knocked him out before he knocked me out."

So much for truth, justice, and the American way, virtues King trumpets loudly and incessantly, even whilst in Japan. If either Jose Sulaiman of the WBC or Gilberto Mendoza of the WBA, dismisses Douglas's apparent victory, it would be the equivalent of Peter Ueberroff voiding the results of the 1985 World Series because umpire Don Denkinger missed a call at first base in game six.

Not since Jack Dempsey's manager/promoter Doc Kearns set out to relieve the good citizens of Shelby, Montana, of their hard-earned money in the 1923 title fight, has a boxing man attempted such a bold scam.

And if King were to succeed, Tyson might well become the unwitting victim. How pathetic a sight it would be then, this macho champion propped up by the transparent rulings of over-fed bureaucrats beholden to King.

Maybe Don King thought he could pull off this travesty because the fight was held on the other side of the planet in Tokyo, Japan. Maybe the fight didn't seem real in that foreign place; it sure didn't sound like a normal heavyweight championship fight. Maybe King didn't think anyone actually saw the champ get his butt kicked. But people *did* see the fight and, more important, this time the press wasn't going to sit still for King's bullying tactics.

Finally, King saw the light. On February 13—three days after Douglas knocked out Tyson—King held a press conference in Manhattan ending his attempt to strip Douglas of the title. He even had the nerve to deny he had ever tried to change the result, explaining that he was just stirring things up for a rematch. And to make what the entire planet already knew official the WBC, the WBA, and the IBF all finally recognized James "Buster" Douglas as the undisputed heavyweight champion of the world. Shame on them all.

HBO did a follow-up show on the contested long count. It was good and proper that they would air this controversy. But of course, the one person who should've been in the studio with the rest of the players was conspicuously missing—Don King.

The world was sitting at Buster Douglas's feet. When Roman soldiers came home from far away military triumphs they were feted to a grand parade through Rome. The streets would be lined with cheering Roman citizens. In golden chariots, the honored heroes were treated like gods. And in the chariot behind each soldier stood a lone slave whispering in his ear, "Fame is fleeting."

It's one thing to prepare both mentally and physically for a great sports event, it's something altogether different to prepare for what comes after. The next thing Buster knew he was the prime guest on both the *Larry King Show* and *David Letterman*. One day he's some nobody from the Blackburn Gym in Columbus, Ohio, the next day he's talking to millions of Americans on national television. While watching this man facing his newfound fame, it would soon become clear that Buster Douglas was something much different from what we had come to expect from the modern boxing world. Buster was a sincere and good man. He wasn't the brilliant showman of Muhammad Ali, or the distant,

impassive George Foreman (the early George Foreman) and certainly not the dark persona of a Mike Tyson. This was evident
even when Buster tried to be something he wasn't, like when he
posed, mouth gaped, (à la Muhammad Ali) for the cameras immediately after his title fight in Tokyo. This was never clearer
than his performances on the talk-show circuit. Suddenly we had
a gentleman champion, a champion for the common man. Buster
Douglas was on the brink of altering the image of an entire sport.
In the end perhaps that's too much to ask of a man.

22

LARRY KING

On February 18, 1990, one week after his triumph in Japan, Buster Douglas, new world heavyweight boxing champion, appeared on the *Larry King Show*. Where does a fighter get the confidence, King wanted to know, to go up against Mike Tyson—an undefeated fighter, never even knocked down, sometimes defeating opponents before the fight begins? King added that he wouldn't have expected a fighter like Buster to have that confidence going into a fight like this.

Buster seemed very much at ease in the TV studio atmosphere, like he'd been rehearsing for the gig for a long time. Buster would answer that he had all the faith and courage and belief in the world when he went into the ring that night. He had accepted the challenge wholeheartedly and intended to do his best to make the dream come true, that dream being to take the title away from Tyson. King wondered how Buster had planned to take command of the fight, something that had to happen if Buster were to win, and whether Tyson had any surprises for him during the fight.

Buster paid his dutiful tribute to Tyson at this point, expressing his admiration at his championship run, but allowed that there were really no surprises from the champ. He quickly corrected himself stating that, in fact, he was stunned at Tyson's ability to take such a pounding for so many rounds. The entire Douglas team gained respect for Mike Tyson that afternoon. Buster continued saying that he relied on something his father taught him: when a guy is a strong thrower, especially a man over 200 pounds, keep working in the ring, don't get excited, and, most importantly, stick to the game plan. That's exactly what Buster did, although he admitted to King that he did become angry when

Tyson knocked him down in the eighth round. No, he wasn't hurt when he hit the canvas, he was angry because he had committed the cardinal sin with Tyson of leaning over and opening himself up. When that happened, Tyson—who is short—jumped down and lunged at Buster with everything he had. This knocked Buster off balance, and the momentum from Tyson's punch sent him stumbling backward and eventually he hit the mat. At that point in the interview, King laughed and told Buster he knew could clearly tell Buster was mad after watching the tape of the knockdown. King then attempted to get a further reaction from the new champ by reminding him that Tyson had literally never been knocked down. Buster calmly smiled at King and told him he wasn't surprised that he put the champ on the canvas because he knew the extent of his arsenal of punches even though the experts and analysts didn't. Buster semi-playfully added that none of the analysts and so-called experts had ever been in the ring with him.

At this point in the interview King reminded Buster that, regardless of his power, Buster had lost four fights. How did that happen? Buster didn't hesitate and responded that he was just "getting through the building." "When you're working hard over a period of time, building your game, not everything works all the time. You've got to find out what works for you, but the main thing is to stick to your guns and believe in yourself." So, he must have been doing something right, Buster added, to be on national television, the undisputed world heavyweight champion.

King would then move on to the confusing and unbelievable post-fight reports that had been circulating since the Tokyo surprise. Evander Holyfield was already under contract to fight Tyson after Japan, but of course, Buster voided that contract. Now, the question everybody wanted to know, who and when would Buster be fighting next? Adding to the confusion was the fact that Holyfield had been the number-one contender and was expected to be fighting Tyson after he had his way with Douglas. Now Douglas and his team were in the boxing driver's seat. Douglas put it in his own words, "They had counted me out; I was just a stepping stone. It turns out that stepping stone was a lion."

Buster did not intend, he told King, to fight again until September, preferring, as he put it, to "bask in the glory of being James Douglas" for the time being. King agreed that this was certainly something he was entitled to and then asked about endorsements, commercials, and appearances. Douglas quickly replied that those things were exactly what he was talking about—just reaping those benefits. It had been a long, hard road for the man from Columbus, Ohio.

King would turn back to the next fight. He wanted to know where the fight might take place, adding that Donald Trump had expressed interest in promoting a fight sometime in June in Atlantic City. Buster was noncommittal, stating he liked both Atlantic City and Las Vegas, but actually the fight could be held anywhere—wherever the highest bidder turned out to be.

King also wondered whether Douglas expected to get the higher end of the purse if a rematch with Tyson were approved— the answer from Buster was an unequivocal yes. Buster had made history, beating the guy who was supposed to be invincible. Buster was now the world champion. Absolutely he'd be getting the lion's share of the purse—no question in Buster's mind.

King summed it up: "The fight would be in September, but we don't know where yet, and Don King has the contract?" "Not so simple," Buster replied—"yes and no." It seemed that Don King was representing both parties, but that a third party could promote the fight. Buster's take, though, was that there was some dispute as to whether King did in fact represent both fighters at this time, saying that he was questioning the current situation. Larry King then went for the jugular: Was Buster trying to remove himself from his current contract with Don King? In a calm, stern response, Buster indicated a lot would have to change to keep him with Don King—Don King would have to show more concern for James Douglas than he currently was. Larry King speculated that maybe Don King had been in the Tyson orbit exclusively and that had hurt Douglas. Buster thought about this insight for a moment, and then replied that it hadn't hurt him in the beginning—that King had been fair, if a bit distant. Tyson was the man after all. But after their last meeting it had all started getting to him—penetrating in ways that it never had before, and he had mentioned it to his manager, John Johnson, who in turn expressed Buster's feelings to King. Now, Buster and Johnson were just waiting to see what would come out of that meeting.

King was then ready to take phone calls and introduce the viewing audience to James "Buster" Douglas, undisputed heavyweight champion of the world, winner of what is generally acknowledged as the biggest upset in boxing history. The first caller wanted to know how it was possible that one of the judges had Tyson ahead on the card, and was Douglas shocked when he first heard of this. Buster, without elaborating on the point, simply said no. King interrupted to ask Buster if the two fighters talked at all during the fight. Again Douglas said no. The next caller said that he was very happy that Buster won the fight, adding that he lived just two blocks from Tyson and that Tyson was a very cocky individual. He also wanted to know whether Tyson's punches felt like bricks and whether they hurt him. No again. Buster said that the best defense is a good offense, and that his was to throw his punches before Tyson's. He knew Tyson had good speed, but as Buster put it, he could shoot into the wind. King added here that during the fight Douglas threw and landed twice as many punches as Tyson. Buster agreed.

King then moves to a more personal subject for Buster—the death of his beloved mother on January 19, just two weeks before the fight. King went on to acknowledge the fact that she and Buster were extremely close and wanted to know how her loss affected Buster's performance, adding that for some people it might have been a very negative thing to deal with. He asked Buster if he would talk about it. Buster didn't hesitate to respond to the personal question. Buster explained that he had a total belief in Jesus Christ and that he knew Christ would not have let him come that far just to let him down. King also asked whether Buster believed his mother had seen the fight or was aware of it—did he have that kind of faith? There was, Buster responded, absolutely no question at all. Buster says he knew she was "up there" driving people crazy, telling them that was her baby down there. Buster's mother was a strong woman—she was the one who raised the kids, while their father was out earning a living. She was the real fighter in the family and Buster doesn't doubt for one minute whether she knows that he is the heavyweight champion of the world.

King took another call. The caller wanted to know if Buster went into the ring with the intention of hurting Tyson. Buster explained, "I went out there to establish control of the fight. You know, getting off first, not hesitating to see what he was going to do, but to get my shots off first and take it from there. Never lose control." King then asked to if Buster was ever afraid. Never, said Douglas. He feared no man other than Jesus Christ. Anybody else is simply a man like himself, and the man he met in the ring in Tokyo got knocked out.

King concluded the interview telling the audience what a great champion Columbus, Ohio had, again speculating on who Douglas might be fighting come September and reminding everyone that the ball was now very much in Buster's court.

23

LETTERMAN

John Johnson reflects back on the David Letterman show: "We were staying right on Central Park at Park Avenue in New York City. My wife, Sue, and I watched the Letterman show in our hotel suite. We had seen it taped earlier that evening. I had come up with the idea for James to wear the championship belt under his suit coat. When James walked out on that stage and he sat down and opened up his coat to show off the belt the crowd went absolutely nuts. I began to cry. I think it was at that point everything that had happened finally caught up with me. I just lost it. It had only been a couple of days since Tokyo and it was the first time I could relax with my wife. And then to see James come on national TV and hear that audience cheer, it just caught up with me."

Later that evening Don King would track Johnson down in his suite. He offered Johnson and Douglas $10 million for a rematch with Tyson. Johnson told King that given what he had done to James after the fight, as far as he was concerned King was now on the same playing field as anybody else and Johnson would go with whoever offered him the best deal. He then told King he had already received phone calls for more money than King just offered. King was not happy. As he left the hotel room King turned to Johnson and said, "Well, Johnny, you go after that fantasy money; and when you can't get it, you come back to me and we'll talk."

Isn't it amazing how dreams really do come true?

David Letterman observed that not everyone could wear a tailored grey suit with a belt like the one Buster was wearing for the show. Buster beamed as he sat down next to Letterman, his

new belt sparkling under the studio lights. Letterman congratulated the new champ and asked which belt he was wearing—and
weren't there more belts, or are all the titles in one belt? Buster
explained that the belt he was currently wearing was the IBF belt,
the only sanctioning body that recognized him as the champion
immediately after the fight.

Letterman again congratulated Buster and speculated that
this must be, no doubt, the best time of Buster's life. Buster
beamed. "It's been a long time coming," he said. Buster then added
that he started chasing his dream at age 10, fighting amateurs
until he was 15. He then started playing other sports, basketball,
football, and baseball, thus moving away from boxing. But he
returned to the sport of his father and turned professional in
1981.

Letterman then asked about Buster's thoughts going into the
fight, whether he had any doubts about beating Tyson. Was he
thinking, "do I have a chance?" or, "there's no point even putting
on the trunks"?

Buster told Letterman that there was never a time when he
didn't think he had an outstanding chance in the fight. He said
that he knew he would go into the ring and do what was necessary to win. Letterman pushes Douglas; he wanted the champ to
elaborate on what those things that led to neutralizing and defeating Tyson were. "Focus and power," Buster said. "Focus and
power." He added that sticking to the movements that he knew
worked for him was important.

"Stick to the movements," Letterman repeated. "Now, he
knocked you down, right?"

"Yes," answered Buster.

"OK, now what round was that?" asked Letterman.

"Eighth round."

"That was the controversial long count, right?"

"Right," Buster answered.

Letterman then wanted to know who times the count, whether
it's the referee in the ring or somebody ringside. Buster told him
the referee is in charge of the two fighters in the ring at all times

and it was to him (the referee) that Buster looked to pick up the count. When he was dropped by Tyson's uppercut to the chin, he knew he wasn't really hurt; it was more like being knocked off balance and pushed, remaining completely coherent. Buster elaborated, explaining that the fight tape shows he slammed the canvas with his gloved hand and said, "Daggone!"

Letterman pressed Buster, "You knew you weren't hurt and that you could continue, so you're using the ten count to kinda gather yourself."

Letterman was interrupted at this point when Douglas reminded him that if a fighter doesn't get up before the count of 10, the fight is over. The audience laughed at this and Letterman smiled. "I picked up the count at six," Buster continued. "Instead of jumping straight up I waited until seven, and when he was going to eight, I proceeded to get up." Letterman clarified here as to whether the referee was looking at a watch and Buster told him no, it's just a count, not necessarily an actual 10 seconds. That was what, according to Buster, caused the big deal about the long count. Some people were saying it was 14 seconds or so and that he got extra time to regroup. Letterman seems intrigued, and asked what would happen if the referee counted really fast. Buster smiled and agreed, indicating that there is a timekeeper at ringside who was already at the count of four when the referee started at one. Letterman said this should be discounted because of the human factor, and Buster agreed.

Letterman asked who made the big fuss in the first place—was it Don King, Mike Tyson, or both? Buster, without hesitation, told Letterman that it was actually Don King. Letterman acted surprised, wondering why he made such a big stink about this. Buster refused to get into the obvious reasons why King might want to submarine Buster's career. In classic Letterman form, he asked Buster if he'd like to know what he thought. Buster took the bait and said yes. "He's a baby," said Letterman, and the crowd erupted with loud cheering. Buster smiled and Letterman thanked the crowd and then jokingly asked if someone would be willing to drive him home.

The interview continued with Letterman suggesting that perhaps Don King could get something done about his hair. He continued asking Buster to elaborate on the fateful 10th round and the eventual knock out of Tyson. Was Tyson hurt during the fight? Buster said he thought he was. Buster explained in a proud manner that after he was knocked down in the eighth he came back hard in the ninth. Tyson was on the ropes and Douglas missed a couple of shots that he thought would have finished Tyson off a round earlier.

"Rights or lefts?" Letterman asked.

"Rights," Buster answered succinctly.

"Is that your money punch?" Letterman pressed.

Buster told his host that that his money punch could come from either hand, and Letterman was obviously impressed with the response. He then wanted to know, as Larry King did in the earlier interview, whether Buster and Tyson talked to each other during the fight—anything nasty said to each other? "Nah," said Buster. "And after the fight?" Letterman pressed. "No, he left the room." Buster added that Tyson told him later that he tried to come over to him in the ring to congratulate him but it was just too crowded.

Letterman said he heard that Douglas does a Tyson impression, true or false? Buster denied this. Letterman said it was probably not a good idea to admit it, even if it were true, and then said that he himself did not watch the fight, that he was long asleep when the fight began. But he said after the fight he was listening to radio call-ins and people were saying that nobody was watching Tyson fights anymore, that he could not find anybody worthy to fight, and no one was spending money to watch his fights. Letterman speculated that this was a manipulation to regenerate interest in Tyson's career and wanted to know what Douglas thought.

Buster replied that he went into the ring to do his job and succeeded in doing what no other man had done before him. He had the opportunity and he made the best of it. Letterman mentioned that they weren't giving odds on the fight in Vegas, and

Buster said he knew that, but he also knew that if he applied him-self he'd have no problem with Tyson.

Letterman next wanted to know what Buster thought the future would hold. Would Buster go out and fight some bums, have a fight once a month, make as much money as possible, and turn lights out right and left? Buster said he couldn't do that because he wouldn't be motivated enough to apply himself in the fights—one thing he learned about boxing is that he needs a challenge.

The big challenge, Letterman speculated, would be a Tyson-Douglas rematch.

Buster immediately responded that it might be a fight against the number-one challenger, Evander Holyfield. Whoever came up with the most money would most likely get the fight, he specu-lated. Letterman noted that Buster's situation was the quintessen-tial American "Rocky" dream, except in Buster's case he knocked out the champion. Letterman saw immediately that Buster did not like the analogy. Without skipping a beat Letterman quickly told Buster it was not his idea, but that of his producer—the skinny kid over in the corner. "See, that's him right there. Look at him, he can't even make a fist, that guy," said Letterman as the camera panned to the show's producer, who was off camera. "We'll get him first," Buster laughed.

Letterman looked at Douglas and reminded him that he's the heavyweight champion of the world. Buster just shook his head and told Letterman that it really had not sunk in yet. He told the audience a story about going through the airport for the first time after the fight. People were all over him, just wanting to get close to him. It was overwhelming.

Concluding the interview, Letterman again congratulated Douglas on the title, saying he couldn't be happier and wishing him good luck, whatever he does.

24

A HOMETOWN
CELEBRATION

They're hanging from the rafters…
> —Dana Tyler, Channel 10 News

Buster Douglas returned home a hero. The *American Heritage Dictionary* lists three definitions for the word hero. "1. In legend, a man celebrated for his bold exploits. 2. A person noted for feats of courage or nobility of purpose. 3. A person noted for special achievement in a particular field." James "Buster" Douglas fits all three definitions.

Columbus, Ohio has had its share of heroes. Whether in the field of medicine, science, education, or sports, especially sports, Columbus takes a backseat to no other city. And Buster Douglas takes a backseat to no other hero. So, why *did* Buster capture us in such a special way? Why did the city come pouring out for Buster Douglas after his triumph in Tokyo like no other hometown star before him? Perhaps it simply comes down to a combination of where he came from, the sport he chose, and the ultimate drama of how he got to the top of his sport. I mean, the great Jack Nicklaus claims Columbus as his home; this, the man who dominated his sport like no other, the man Tiger Woods has dreamed his entire life of becoming. Columbus would build a sterile, empty museum for Jack; for Buster, its citizens would embrace him in the streets of their city. Why the difference? Is it because Nicklaus grew up in a privileged environment (Upper Arlington—a suburb of Columbus) and played a privileged sport? A white man's game that's performed on gated and perfectly manicured outdoor cathedrals, its single goal to push a tiny ball into a small hole in the ground while surrounded by fans who, if they utter a single inappropriate sound at an inappropriate moment, may be summarily ejected from the premises. Buster Douglas sprung from the streets of the inner city and reached the pinnacle of a sport that resides in rowdy, smoke-filled arenas located in seedy cities like Las Vegas and Atlantic City and has a single goal of ripping the head off an opponent who is trapped inside a 20 by 20 foot space, enclosed by ropes. Whatever the reason, the city of Columbus, Ohio opened up its arms like never before or since.

❐　❑　❐

Clark Donley, Channel 6 News, Columbus, Ohio: And here at Windsor Terrace, Windsor Community Center, James "Buster" Douglas has just been announced to the crowd as he steps on stage.
[*The crowd chants "BUSTER! BUSTER!"*]
K. C. Jones, WVKO Radio: Ladies and gentlemen, introducing the gentleman who has given us the biggest upset in boxing history. He has changed the way people will look at Columbus, Ohio, where James "Buster" Douglas is from! Not only will this be Windsor Terrace, this is going to be Windsor Terrace where Buster Douglas grew up. We're gonna talk to Buster in a minute, but I want to introduce to you the Honorable Mayor of Columbus, Mayor Rinehart.
Mayor Dana "Buck" Rinehart: Buster Douglas, Columbus loves you. Somebody from CBS asked me, "What does Buster Douglas mean to Columbus?" I said, "That's easy, he's our hero." He loves Columbus, and we're proud of him. Where is Mike Tyson? Still on his back! Ladies and gentlemen, I give you our friend, our neighbor, the heavyweight champion of the world, James "Buster" Douglas!
Buster Douglas: I'd like to thank everybody for coming out and showing their support and appreciation. It's

an honor and I just can't express how great I feel. Coach John Johnson's team has come a long way. Without the help of my manager, John Johnson, I wouldn't be here today. [Buster starts to get emotional.] I'll turn it over to John.

John Johnson: When I came here today I didn't know I was going to talk. But every day I have a different feeling about what's happening. My thoughts this morning are with Buster. James Douglas is not only the heavyweight champion he's the *best* heavyweight champion *ever*! Thank you very much.

Dana Tyler, Channel 10 News: Another reason why this is so important for this neighborhood is that this is a place that has had some problems. They admit it, problems with drugs and alcohol, with gang violence. In a lot of cases you can look right out the windows and see people selling crack. But a lot that's going on inside the school and inside the recreation center are positive things. For example, they have a boxing program here that has been going on for a long time. In fact, Buster Douglas's father, Bill "Dynamite" Douglas, trained here; Buster trained at the Blackburn Center. Boxing has been so important, not only because it has helped people like Buster, but it helps little kids; makes them feel proud of themselves and it also gives them something to shoot for because of what happened to Buster Douglas.

There is a special presentation for Buster Douglas from *USA Today*—look at that, they're holding up a plaque—it's a replica of Monday's paper with Buster's picture on the front page, it's a special edition printed just for Buster Douglas.

Look who's here now, it's Dick Gregory, known all over the country for his great community work.

Dick Gregory, civil rights activist, and animal rights activist: I'd just like to say behind every great person

there's a great family—great friends, great neighborhood, great city, great state, and most of all, a great God.

Lou Forrest, Channel 6 News: We probably should mention that a part of the pictures from today's downtown
parade that are being sent out to everyone in our Channel 6 viewing area is also going out to ESPN, also to
ABC, and a lot of home satellite dish wires as well.

Michelle Gailiun, Channel 6 News: I think the world is
watching.

Lou Forrest: The world is watching literally. Let's go to
the tape, Michelle.

[*The TV screen cuts to videotape.*]

Narrator: Despite what the world might think, Buster
Douglas didn't just appear out of nowhere. His quest
for the world heavyweight title actually began nearly
a decade ago. Following in the footsteps of his father, Bill "Dynamite" Douglas, a former middleweight contender, Buster first set out to win the
championship for his dad, the championship which,
for so many years, had eluded him.

Buster Douglas: That's one of the reasons why I'm fighting professionally, my dad. I wanted to do something
that he didn't really get a chance to do. I just wanted
to do what he didn't achieve and become heavyweight
champion of the world.

Narrator: During those early years, Buster and his father were a team: Bill the experienced teacher, Buster
the eager student.

Bill "Dynamite" Douglas: It's hard because I'm feeling
this way like any father, but also who'd been a fighter.
I know what it's all about; I know there are rough
blows; I know it's a rough game.

Narrator: Over the years, though, their relationship in
the ring grew rocky; and, by 1987, Buster's father
was no longer in his son's corner. He was, though,
still Buster's biggest fan.

Bill "Dynamite" Douglas: Well, I knew his abilities; I knew what he could do, I knew he had the desire. And he wanted it, so there was really no obstacles.

Narrator: Now Buster's road to the title included some serious peaks and valleys. He hit rock bottom in 1984 when, with an impressive record of 19-2, he ran into Dave Starkey. The fight turned into an embarrassment and was eventually called a draw. Buster was quick to rebound. Exactly four months to the day later, with manager John Johnson now on the inside, he upset former heavyweight contender, Tex Cobb, in a nationally televised fight from Las Vegas. The surge continued, as another four months later, live on ESPN, Douglas once again fell from the limelight, losing a devastating 10-round decision to Jesse Ferguson. It wasn't until eight months later that Buster returned to the ring, his opponent former world champion Greg Page. Just like the Tyson fight, Buster was a heavy underdog; but Douglas dominated the bout and came away with a stunning 10-round decision.

Buster Douglas: After that, we were looking for a title shot. We were told by Don King that if we win the two next fights he'd be glad to give us a title shot; keep winning and we would deserve it.

Narrator: Buster would go on to win two more fights before finally reaching the threshold, a title bout with Tony Tucker for the IBF world heavyweight crown. Tucker walked away with the championship, leaving Buster to start all over again. Following a six-month layoff, Buster returned to score a devastating second-round knockout over Donny Long. He followed that victory with five more wins, including three by way of knockout. Finally in July of 1989, after beating Oliver McCall in Atlantic City, Douglas and his manager Johnson were ready for their dream fight.

John Johnson: The dream is just to have James Douglas win the world title within the next year.

[*Tape stops.*]

Lou Forrest: I could watch that tape over and over again. Right now, we're going up for a live picture from Sky-6 and see how this parade is shaping up.

Michelle Gailiun: Wow, all you can see is people. This is really exciting, the crowds are really picking up behind us now.

Doug Lessells, Channel 4 News, interviewing Jerry Page: Jerry, John Johnson came on board six years before the big fight. Actually, Douglas sought out Johnson. How big of an impact did Johnson have on James's career?

Jerry Page: Well, it turned out to be a big impact. James Douglas ended up in two championship fights after he picked John Johnson as his manager. John Johnson obviously did all the right things in terms of getting in the right fights and getting him on the right cards. So now he's got a world champion.

Angela Pace, Channel 4 News: So he was able then to overcome these personal problems and also get himself positioned with the right people around him and that was the key to his success.

Jerry Page: That's true. With professional boxers a lot of things take place that people don't see. The manager's always working on the fighter's behalf, and if he can make the right moves and contact the right people, some great things can happen.

Angela Pace: Thank you very much, Jerry. Now things have been very busy for Buster Douglas, especially in the two weeks after the big fight. He has spent very little time here in his hometown. He's been traveling quite a bit. But right before he left for Tokyo, Doug Lessells spent a long day with Buster.

Doug Lessells: The anticipation started out with his

training and continued with some local pep rallies, then, you're right Angela, it turned into a pretty long day for James Douglas.

[The TV screen cuts to a second videotape.]

Narrator: It was a heavyweight day for the heavyweight contender James Douglas. Up at 7:30 A.M. for a five-mile run. At 10:30 Douglas was at the gym to shoot a public service announcement for the multiple sclerosis society. And at 2:00, James visited the Windsor Elementary School for a send-off rally.

Cheerleaders: 2, 4, 6, 8; who do we appreciate? *Douglas, Douglas, Douglas!*

Buster Douglas: That brought back a lot of memories. Looking out at those kids, I could see myself out there at that age. That was great. That is one thing I tend to focus on is youth because they're our tomorrow. I enjoy working with kids.

Narrator: The final this afternoon was a skit performed by two of the Windsor students imitating Mike Tyson and James Douglas. Guess who won?

[Tape stops.]

Angela Pace: And that is one of my favorite stories leading up to the Buster Douglas triumph. Now, his flight to Tokyo and then his moment of destiny began at very early hour about two weeks ago with a 7:30 A.M. flight out of Port Columbus. Doug Lessells was the only Columbus television reporter who was there for the send-off.

[Back to the videotape.]

Narrator: It's a mission Mr. Douglas has already chosen to accept: to become the first man to beat world heavyweight champion Mike Tyson in thirty-seven professional bouts. Contrary to what the fight experts are predicting, the Douglas camp doesn't consider it a mission impossible.

Buster Douglas: It's been a long time coming, man;

I'm past due, and I want to make the best of my opportunity.

John Johnson: We're living the ultimate dream, and we're going to win the heavyweight championship of the world. And we're ready to go.

Buster Douglas: My work is behind me; we're just going to taper down and start getting really focused on what we're going to do—what I'm gonna do—when I get there.

Doug Lessells: And what's that?

John Johnson: James Douglas is going to knock Mike Tyson out. That's what we're going there for.

Doug Lessells: Stay tuned for the exciting conclusion! [*Tape stops.*]

Angela Pace: John Johnson sounded like he knew exactly what he was talking about. He was so *definite* about it.

Doug Lessells: I'll tell you what, Mr. Graves: that was no *Mission Impossible.* They knew they were going to go out there and knock Mike Tyson out. And, you know, all the way through the build-up to it, Angela, they weren't talking about going over there and just making a good showing, about not getting hurt. They were talking about knocking out Tyson. And they went over and did it.

Angela Pace: What was interesting, right after you did that story, you were on *Evening News Watch* at seven o'clock; and even *you* were saying that you had a real good feeling about what James Douglas was going to be able to do.

Doug Lessells: I did, because everybody said that Mike Tyson's invincible. But Tyson has never faced a boxer with James's qualifications and James's ability. He's a big, strong guy: 6-4, 230 pounds. Mike Tyson's 5-11—a short, compact guy who needs to get inside. Everybody else—those 33 guys that Mike Tyson knocked out—let him get inside, Angela. And you could tell that James had a good strategy: keep him away from Buster with jabs and tie him up when he came in close. They had a plan that looked like it would work, and it did work.

Angela Pace: And not just a lot of technical skill, he was a man on a mission.

Doug Lessells: Oh, yeah!

Angela Pace: Definitely motivated. We're going to go back live now to the parade staging area at downtown Broad and Grant. You can see that the folks are starting to get a little excited there. They sense that the beginning of the parade is near.

[*Channel 6 News Videotape*]

Jim Day, Channel 6 News, voiceover: After meeting Buster Douglas, you do walk away with the feeling that you have just met a genuinely nice guy, a man with his feet on the ground, humble in his actions. Even right after the fight, he was still the same person.

Buster Douglas: I did it all for my mother, I did it for my team—Coach Boxing, and for my son and dad.

Jim Day: And when he arrived home from Tokyo, it was the kids he first thanked.

Buster Douglas: I'd like to thank all the little people, all the kids who went to alternative school. I'd like to thank everybody for coming out. I appreciate it.

Jim Day: James "Buster" Douglas has put Columbus on the map, shedding a spiritual light upon our city. We are giving dignity back to the heavyweight championship. Just what boxing needed.

Michelle Gailiun: OK, these guys are being mobbed. The police are trying to have everybody stand back, but people don't want to. They want to get close to Buster; they want to feel a part of this.

Lou Forrest: The parade has actually started, I believe.

Michelle Gailiun: They're moving right beside us, right now.

Lou Forrest: Great. We're just going to turn and look over here ourselves—we have a truck with television cameras on it down there. The police are having a hard time because the crowd is just surging in as Buster Douglas comes by.

Michelle Gailiun: They're throwing flowers and all sorts of things here. There is so much more to this parade, but right now the focus is James "Buster" Douglas. We're going to hear from the Linden-McKinley marching band; that should be fun. Linden, of course is Buster's alma mater. Right now the throngs are just staying with him as much as possible.

Dana Tyler, [*introducing a new videotape*]: We got the chance to meet Buster earlier and it was a thrill for us. I was impressed with just how normal he was and just what a nice guy he was.

[*Videotape showing Buster playing high school basketball*]

Narrator: Do you remember this, Buster?

Buster Douglas: The basketball champs of Linden-McKinley. That was a big, big day for us, man. We won the state championship—baddest team in the land. I've been a champion all my life! I've been associated with champions all my life; most people don't know that. The boxing critics, they don't know anything about that. The only thing they go by is what they see in the ring. That's why they called the fight an upset. We never doubted my abilities. We never doubted I'd go in there and do the right things and apply myself accordingly and that I'd take Mike Tyson out. I've been a champion all my life—and associated with champions all my life.

[*Tape stops.*]

Bob Orr, Channel 10 News: That video was from 12 years ago. Things were a little bit different then. James Douglas was a reserve forward on that high school championship team. He was not the star of the show, but he certainly is the star of the show today. Last night at the Columbus Touchdown Club, Jerry Revish used a line that has stuck with me. He said that in years past, James Douglas couldn't have afforded a ticket to the Touchdown Club, and last night he owned the place.

Dana Tyler: All eyes were on him at the Touchdown Club. Buster also said to us last night that one thing that was really important for him was that he was a role model in person for the kids here in Columbus. He wasn't just somebody from another city that they could look up to and not really know personally, but he was somebody right here. And that's why he is in the parade today, enjoying himself despite the fact that he forgot his gloves on this cold day—he could've worn his boxing gloves!

Bob Orr: If you're looking carefully at your television screen and you see that earphone dangling from the champ's right ear, that was our attempt to have Buster talk back directly with us. But he is so absolutely overwhelmed with the people around him that that's proven to be impossible. It's been an exciting time downtown today, and I think the champ is cherishing the moment. He is in no particular hurry to get down to City Hall. When he does get here, however, I want to tell you that he's going to find a whale of a crowd of people.

Dana Tyler: They're hanging from the rafters.

Bob Orr: They have literally closed down Front Street in front of City Hall. I'm not sure how the parade is going to make its way around City Hall, but we're told the ceremony will start here around noon straight up.

Angela Pace: It now looks as though the people along the parade route have become part of the parade themselves. They're not content just to stand along Broad

Street and cheer Buster Douglas on. They have become part of the processional, they're handing him flowers and are working their way also down Broad Street so they can take part in the celebration here at City Hall.

Buster Douglas has become pretty much an overnight success; and the original Rocky himself, Sylvester Stallone, wants to do a movie on the Buster Douglas story, but he's going to have to stand in line. Buster's manager, John Johnson, says that it's going to take some money—everyone wants a piece of the champ; but it could be millions of dollars as far as the price tag goes. Jim Schroeder has this report.

[*TV cuts to a videotape.*]

Jim Schroeder, Channel 10 News: Believe it or not, John Johnson had to go hat in hand to PONY and ask them to give him shorts, a robe, and shoes for Buster to wear in the Tyson fight. But you can believe that, for the next fight, someone is going to pay James Douglas to wear equipment. Experts believe the contract could be worth more than a million dollars. Nike has already contacted Johnson about an endorsement package, and dozens of other companies want to put Buster's name on their products. It is estimated that Buster Douglas can make 10 to 20 million dollars on endorsements alone before he ever fights again. But his manager and financial adviser, John Johnson, is saying they will be very selective. Buster will not endorse alcohol or tobacco products. He will market himself as the clean-cut people's champ, more of a Wheaties type. Tyson has sold the image of a tough, brash champion to, among others, Nintendo. Is there anything in particular Buster Douglas wants to see his face on?

Buster Douglas: Maybe my own cartoon.

[*Tape stops.*]

Angela Pace: He wants his own cartoon. Jerry, how marketable is Buster Douglas going to be now?

Jerry Page: I think John Johnson made a great decision by moving any rematch back just to see how marketable James Douglas is. He's appeared on a lot of national television shows, and I think that's going to be a boost to his marketability. I think he'll make several millions of dollars. He's already hit it here in Columbus—he'll be big here for the rest of his life—but it's yet to be seen on a national level."

Angela Pace: OK, so you think it was a wise decision not to do any kind of rematch in June but to push it back to, at the very earliest, September so that he could take advantage of all the publicity over the next several months?

Jerry Page: Oh, yes, there's no doubt about it. He needs to get out there and get it done because you never know what can happen in the next fight, whoever it's against; he might not win again.

Angela Pace: It is high noon; it is Buster Douglas Day here in Columbus, Ohio. You can hear over the loudspeakers they have started the celebration. Buster Douglas is on his way up to the grandstand. There are a lot of people who have brought their children here today to get a look at what may be their only look at a heavyweight world champion.

Bob Orr: Buster Douglas and John Johnson have raised the point about the potential of a fight in Ohio Stadium. Is that really likely or not? No, it's not likely. Is it a potential? Absolutely. Here's the deal: John Johnson was telling us last night and all through the week, whoever comes up with the best financial backing . . .

Dana Tyler, Channel 10 News: Money, money, money.

Bob Orr: The best television package will probably be in Las Vegas, Atlantic City, or Ohio Stadium. I'm talking about a rematch with Mike Tyson. Of course, there are a lot of variables, mainly Evander Holyfield, the number one contender, who wants a piece of this action, and Don King—and this is noteworthy—Don King, Mike Tyson's manager says, "I'm a Buckeye; I'll fight in Ohio Stadium. Put up the purse. Buster's the champ; if he says 'be there,' we'll be there."

Jerry Page: This is unbelievable! You'd think that we were at an Ohio State football game.

Angela Pace: That's exactly what it looks like! They were estimating up to 30,000 people would show up today and it looks like the estimate will be very close. And this is the moment everybody's been waiting for, the introduction of the champ. And there he is! You can see that signature red hat. James "Buster" Douglas is about ready to take the stage. Once he gets there in clear view of everybody here, the place will rock, Jerry.

Jerry Page: That's right. There's his whole boxing staff; there's his main man, John Johnson; look, Johnson's up there jumping all around.

Angela Pace: That's one happy man right there!

Jerry Page: John Johnson—it's a dream come true for him, you know.

Angela Pace: He has to be very proud—very proud. He helped Buster over some rough times, gave him the confidence that he needed, steered him in the right direction, and has been very protective of him since the fight.

Jerry Page: John was saying all along that he was going to have a heavyweight champion; he was saying that Buster Douglas was going to be that champion.

Columbus Mayor, Dana "Buck" Rinehart: I would like Buster's grandmother and son, Lamar, to stand up. These people are also heroes. If you're gonna have a hero, we all want that person to stand for the very best. Buster Douglas worked day and night, week after week, month after month, year after year to have one chance to make a dream come true. Today, Buster, Columbus, Ohio shares your victory. We love your spirit and we love what you stand for. These thousands of people out here are proud you brought "the gold" to Columbus, Ohio.

Ladies and gentlemen, now is the moment you have been waiting for. It gives me a great deal of pleasure, and I'm honored to present to you the undisputed heavyweight champion of the world, James "Buster" Douglas!

Buster Douglas: I'd like to thank everybody for coming out today to show their support and appreciation. It's a great honor and as Mayor Rinehart said earlier, I couldn't have done it without the support of Columbus, my family, and coach John Johnson's team. I love you. It really makes me feel good to see all of you out here today. I just have to thank the Lord Jesus Christ for giving me the strength to weather the storm. Thank you.

Bob Orr: The man on Buster's right is John Johnson, the man we've talked about who's the manager you've heard so much about. Let's go back to Buster.

Buster Douglas: I'd like to introduce the man who's most influential on James Douglas's career, my manager and friend, John Johnson.

John Johnson: Five and a half years ago we sat down in my living room and we talked about a dream. And that dream now has come true. Ladies and gentlemen the people behind me today are a family, a team, a boxing team. Ladies and gentlemen, we love you all. We're just hard-working, honest, God-loving people. And I'll tell you, as James said, the reason we beat Mike Tyson is because we believe in Jesus Christ, we believe in God. And Mike Tyson was just another man; he was just another man. James is now considered the second-most recognizable person in the world and pretty soon he's going to be the most recognizable. Let me make one last point. I believe with all my heart, when I think about all the heavyweight champions that's ever lived, I have no doubt that James Douglas, because of the wonderful, caring person that he is, is the greatest heavyweight champion ever—James "Buster" Douglas. We love you and we love Columbus. Thank you.

DON KING RETURNS

Don King's circus sideshow landed in Columbus, Ohio. Whatever we think about him, one thing is clear. Don King is not a shy man. And maybe more importantly, he will not be ignored. True to his claim that he would "kick Johnson's ass," King's bold post-Tokyo strategy to reinsert himself into the business of "carving up the turkey" was to move his entourage smack into the center of Coach Boxing. His new home? Columbus, Ohio. King didn't come to Columbus without a game plan. Like a wild animal probing his prey for weaknesses, King circled Buster Douglas. He would quickly focus his offensive on two age-old tribal principles, race and fatherhood. The strategy was both brutally shameful and brilliant. How would King exploit his new prey? He would enlist the inner-city black churches and radio stations and pass out hard cash. What Don King did in Buster Douglas's and John Johnson's hometown makes Karl Rove look like an amateur politician. King and Rove are two men from different worlds, but both are brilliant at what they do, and what they do best is win at any cost.

"It was like watching our own soap opera happening in real time right in front of us," Angela Pace, news anchorwoman for Columbus TV station, Channel 4 News, reflecting back after nearly 17 years. "Columbus has never seen anything quite like it before or since." Angela Pace was one of the army of Columbus, Ohio, press that jumped on the sports upset story of the century. Columbus hadn't seen a local story like this in years. All the TV stations were hustling for the best angle on the soap opera.

❐ ❑ ❐

Angela Pace: It's been over a month since Buster Douglas's stunning upset in Tokyo, Japan, and as we told you at the top of the newscast, boxing promoter Don King is in Columbus today to talk with James "Buster" Douglas and to attend Buster Douglas's father's birthday party. We had invited Don King to join us live on *Evening Newswatch*. He accepted our invitation and then later canceled out on us. Don King and Buster Douglas and Buster Douglas's camp have been involved in a feud over Buster Douglas's next fight and over representation of Douglas since the middle of February, right after James Douglas took the heavyweight title away from Mike Tyson. Jim Schroeder has been in basically on the beginnings of this feud since right after that fight in mid-February. Back in New York City, you were there and saw evidence of just how tense the situation was.

Jim Schroeder, Channel 10 News: That's when things really escalated Angela. Ironically, before that John Johnson, Buster Douglas, and Don King had gotten along fine. And Buster Douglas felt Don King was really giving him a chance after he lost the heavyweight title match to Tony Tucker in 1987. Don King kept putting him on undercards and giving him a chance to come back. Buster was appreciative of that. But after the fight, Don King immediately came out and said they can't give him the title because of the long count controversy. That really started the bad blood. Then six days after the fight they all went to HBO for a prior commitment and they showed a replay of the fight. After the replay taping there was a news conference. John Johnson was talking to reporters and Don King came in the room. Let's look at the videotape.

[*TV screen cuts to videotape.*]

John Johnson: None of you treat him like he's the world

champion. You act like he was lucky. He kicked the
guy's ass. He's going to kick it worse the next time—
if there is a next time. I've got an athlete sitting over
there and you're wasting his time. You sat up there
asked Mike Tyson questions: well, Mike, why this;
well, Mike, why that? Mike Tyson got his ass kicked
because he ran into James Douglas. And you guys
all stay married to him! [Johnson points to Tyson]
You all must love him, but he's disrespectful, that's
what he is. And over there [Johnson points to Buster]
is a super nice young man and he doesn't get any
credit. It's the truth. The actions of the people in this
building [HBO] was that Mike Tyson was still the
heavyweight champion. Let's go, James. Thank you
gentleman. James Douglas is the heavyweight champion of the world and he's going to kick Mike Tyson's
ass, and Evander Holyfield, and then go home and
enjoy his family.

Member of the press: In that order?

John Johnson: I don't know if in that order. Buster Douglas has created the biggest boxing show on HBO
history. He created it! Not Mike Tyson!

[*Tape stops.*]

Angela Pace: What did Buster Douglas have to say?

Jim Schroeder: He sat there and said, "Yeah, I agree with
John." But actually, I don't think there was a need to
ask John Johnson how he really feels about Don King.
This is just all a carry-over about Don King representing Mike Tyson's interest and not Buster
Douglas's. Therefore, Johnson and Douglas are arguing that the contract they have with King is null
and void. Obviously, this is all going to be resolved
in the courts.

Angela Pace: And that's exactly where it's going to be
resolved. Any speculation that this is all a put-on, a
hype for the rematch?

Jim Schroeder: No, I really don't think so. I got the impression that John Johnson does not like Don King because of the way Buster Douglas was treated immediately after the fight.

Angela Pace: OK, stay tuned for more on this controversy. Thanks a lot, Jim.

Don King didn't waste any time after arriving in Buster Douglas's hometown. King's first order of business was to attend a birthday party held for Buster's father, Bill "Dynamite" Douglas, and offer a cash "gift" of $10,000. Next, King gave an interview on Columbus inner-city radio station WCKX, where King openly questioned manager John Johnson's ability to do what's best for Buster Douglas because Johnson is white.

> I'm here to see Buster Douglas's father who brought him to me, not John Johnson. I have no problem with John Johnson because John Johnson is acting normal. You must understand that John Johnson is doing nothing abnormal. The first thing they do is try to separate you from your family and your kind; and after they do that, they clone you to do what they want you to do. Hopefully, prayerfully, Buster Douglas won't allow himself to be utilized in that manner. John Johnson calls himself a Christian but he acts like a hypocrite. He told me that he would always be there. He is seeking and looking for excuses to run away, to take the legacy that I have to black people and Hispanics from Muhammad Ali and George Foreman in 1973 and 1974, to take it back to the system, which is a racist institution, to deprive blacks and deny them of opportunity of the right to be compensated for what they do. John Johnson doesn't care nothin' about Buster Douglas. He is just an instrument to be used to further the means of John Johnson and his extreme views.

John Johnson responded in local TV interview. "I do agree with Mr. King, there is prejudice in our world. As a child I was called half-breed because my mother was Indian and Italian. I understand that. But there's none of it here among this group of people. And we will not allow anyone to challenge us on the people that we are."

The station editorialized further on Don King's interview.

Who is Don King to say that John Johnson doesn't care about Buster Douglas? Where was Don King six years ago when Douglas and Johnson started with nothing? Ask Buster Douglas what he thinks about John Johnson; or Buster's trainer, J. D. McCauley; or the Vice President of Buster Douglas, Inc., Rodney Rogers; or the company's accountant—black men all. To say that Buster Douglas is being exploited by John Johnson is a slap at Buster's intelligence. Does Don King think that Buster isn't smart enough to make his own decisions? On the contrary, Don King has made a career of exploiting fighters, and Buster Douglas is too smart to let King to get away with it. Buster is certainly smart enough to see what King is trying to pull with his visit to Columbus, and we can only hope that the people of this community and the rest of the world are as smart as Buster Douglas.

[Don King press conference]
Don King, at a press conference at an inner city church in eastside Columbus: Thank you Reverend Jordan, and I'm certainly appreciative to be in the house of the Lord. You all had a wonderful worship today. And in the spirit of Jesus Christ, my Lord and Savior, I want to express my feelings on the situation that I think is really a very difficult one but is only about one person trying to take another person's rights— and that is Steve Wynn. The person that is really culpable in this situation is not Mr. Johnson, although he's been an instrument in this, and most assuredly

not Mr. Buster Douglas 'cause he don't even understand it. But the man who does understand it is the
owner of the Mirage in Las Vegas. What he did is
take John Johnson on a whirlwind tour plane-ride,
hypnotized him with all of his luxuries, posh el-
egance, offered him all types of smoke-filled numbers to confuse his head and try to take away my
contractual rights. This is what it is all about.

And what he has offered Mr. Johnson, Mr.
Johnson doesn't understand either because he, too,
has never been exposed to anything like this before.
And so, what he is saying—and leading the public to
believe—is that I want to take too much of the pie. I
don't want a dime from Mr. Johnson, nor from his
fighter. I don't have to take anything from them. And
so, Mr. Wynn is confusing Mr. Johnson. Mr. Johnson
will be paid what he's supposed to be paid. And that's
whatever the public brings in, and he gets his fair
share of that, as all before him and after him.

But you must understand that I revolutionized
the pay scale in boxing. Before my advent, they never
got millions in boxing. The highest purses that ever
were paid were to Muhammad Ali and George
Forman at $2.5 million in Madison Square Garden.
When I came in, I gave $5 million to both of them; I
doubled that figure in my first event right out of the
chute. And I think, since that time, my commitment
and mandate has been to helping the black fighter
and the Hispanic fighter who had never got an opportunity, and the white fighter who didn't get no good
chance either—but the white fighters wouldn't come
to a black man—so therefore, the white fighters
were being ripped off by their own. But since I came
into the business, all fighters have gotten a better
price.

One white father brought his whole family to

me—his name is David Hilton—and I made his son champion, Matthew Hilton. So, it's the thing that the fighters do the fighting in the ring, and I do the fighting outside the ring. But when you look at a person like Mr. Wynn, who has the knowledge of what he's trying to do, he's trying to take away my rights. And I'm the guy who extols the virtue of America, not try to knock it down. I decry the iniquities and injustices and seek ways and means to have a better quality of life for all America, for black and white alike, but I'm not going to lay down and let him just take my rights. Johnson says that I'm trying to take something from Buster. This is why he's confused. I'm the guy who carried Buster on my shoulders for nine years, four non-exclusively, five exclusively. I led Buster to the path of being able to put on the championship opportunity, not once but twice.

Member of the press: Aren't you the same man who acted like he didn't recognize Buster after the fight?

Don King: That's not true. This is where they got their presumptions that I didn't recognize Buster. I went over to John Johnson and shook Johnson's hand and congratulated him in the ring, and I went to Buster Douglas, who was very emotional at that particular time. I patted him on the back, and I told him, "Congratulations, champ." Now what they did is they took the perception that I had tried to modify or change the decision. This type of negative perception permeated the country all pervasively. I didn't know this was happening until the time I got off the plane from Tokyo, which is a 14-hour ride. It was like a wildfire in the forest, and it had gotten out of hand. So I had to wait until the time I had opportunity to defend myself. No one can substantiate one fact that I made an official protest, that I tried to modify or change the decision.

Member of the press: What about the press conference in the tape that was shown?

Don King: I didn't speak on it. If you've seen the tape you've seen me sitting there. I am the promoter. And first of all, I invited Mr. Johnson and Mr. Douglas and their attorney to come and be at the press conference when I knew that an official protest had been filed by the Japanese boxing commission. I invited them to be there so I could sit between the two fighters. Then I would have more of a chance to try to speak in a reconciliation situation than I would by not saying anything. But since he wasn't there I didn't open my mouth.

Member of the press: How do you rectify situations like yesterday, for instance, where everyone is getting into a shouting match and nothing's accomplished except more controversy?

Don King: This is something I didn't seek; I'm not inclined to that. What I want to do is sit down with Mr. Johnson—and I'm going to call him. I'm going to call him as soon as I leave this church—and I'm going to sit down and talk with Mr. Johnson. If Mr. Johnson is amenable to sitting down and discussing the situation, I'll most certainly do that because he called me incessantly for five years. And everybody that's closely associated with me, he called. I was there to respond to his plea for help. I supported Mr. Johnson, and I supported Mr. Douglas, completely subsidized them in their boxing career. I paid their expenses; I paid for their opponent; I picked his opponent. I led him down a line, helping him to become an opportunity for heavyweight champion. I gave him that opportunity August 1, 1987, when he fought Tony Tucker. Buster was ahead on all scorecards. His condition left something to be desired, and he ended up getting knocked out. Now, I

told him that he didn't train properly, and I repri-
manded him for not training properly; but then, I also
forgave him for his indiscretion, and I brought him
back for another three-year journey from 1987 to
1990 and gave him another opportunity—exclusively,
all subsidized by me.

As you know, I love Buster. Buster is a good kid.
But Buster never drew anybody to the fight other than
his family. Buster never sold any tickets for me at
any of my promotions. Buster never enhanced one
card. There's not one site in the world that told me,
if I didn't bring Buster to the site, I was going to
have a problem with putting my event there. Buster
has always been there because Don King solely, uni-
laterally, wanted him there. And I did this, now at
the time when the dream has come true, and I . . . I'm
a businessman. I'm a capitalist. I'm in the American
dream. What I do is, I invest in stock. And if you
invest in that stock and it comes to the time for frui-
tion and it declares a dividend, you come and tell me
that I can't collect my dividend, I mean, I don't understand this.

Member of the press: Is that a conflict of interest, though,
to have an interest in both fighters at the same time?
Don King: No, it isn't a conflict of interest. It's a tribute
to my business acumen, to be able to have all fighters coming to me. You must understand that I didn't
invent boxing. When I came into boxing it had become one of the lowest names in the history of mankind. It was corruptible; boxing was racketeering
infiltrated. The image of boxing was that you fix
fights, call decisions, and, if you didn't fight in the
way they wanted you to fight, whoever the cartel rul-
ers were, you didn't fight at all. You had to share
what was in your purse—when you got through to
the end of the day, you didn't have anything. I changed

all that. When I came into the business—if you didn't dance to their music, you couldn't dance—if they had Bach, Beethoven, and Brahms, I just added a little salsa, [and] rhythm and blues. I gave them an alternative. That alternative has proven to be—proven to be—Muhammad Ali. I made more money for Muhammad Ali in the time I promoted him than he did in the whole time of his career. When Muhammad Ali lost his title, I got him another chance to get it back. When he wanted to go out in the evening of his career and fight Larry Holmes, I arranged for him to fight Larry Holmes. When Larry Holmes lost his title, I made him a millionaire. Larry Holmes right now is one of the wealthiest ex-fighters there is: $15 million, a hotel, two office buildings—all with a fourth-grade education. I did that!

Member of the press: Mr. King, are you saying that you are what boxing is today?

Don King: I have revolutionized the pay scale in boxing, and I added a sophistication and a dignity to the sport second to none, by bringing movie stars, dignitaries, chiefs-of-states to the sport, taking and bringing in foreign countries when I couldn't operate in my own home country because of racism and prejudice. A maverick couldn't get to the arena of promoting big fights, even if he's white; a black couldn't get through a porthole. So, I couldn't start in America; I started around the world because I couldn't promote here in America because a black man wasn't allowed to even think of promoting events of that magnitude. So I had to take them to Africa, Malaysia, the Philippines; all around the world I had to go and put on events. After putting on these events of such magnitude and esteem, I was welcomed home like a prodigal son because it was the economics. The money that I was taking to foreign countries, the people in America said they would like to have some of that money here. And I, being a patriot, just left the foreign arena, and came back to my own home country.

But the thing is, I did this with everybody—with Witherspoon, with Larry Holmes, George Forman, Ken Norton, and Roberto Duran. Sugar Ray Leonard is a champion today because I gave him an opportunity. When he lost I gave it back to him.

Member of the press: Why do you need Buster Douglas now?

Don King: Why did I need Buster Douglas seven years ago? Why did I need him five years ago? You know what I mean? It isn't about whether I need Buster Douglas or not, it's that I have rights. The only key question here is my rights. It's the same as you. If you've got a contract with that TV station where you work and after you get to be a network interviewer, then all of a sudden somebody walks in and takes your rights away on your contract, you're just not going to roll over. That's what you earn, that's what you went to journalism school for.

Member of the press: So how do you reconcile?

Don King: Well, you sit down and you talk. The reason that we haven't talked is because John Johnson wouldn't talk. So I'm prayerful and hopeful that he will now.

Member of the press: It seems as if what happened yesterday would be more damaging to Buster here in his own community because now people would look at him and possibly say, "Well, he's a traitor."

Don King: Well, then you have to judge a book, not by its cover, but you must read into the book to find out. You must understand something—my commitment is to black people. You understand? My commitment is to America. As a black American, I stand for black people and to represent myself with equality and strength of a white American. That way you take the burden off of one, and you take the burden off the other so you can sit down at the table of compromise in a democratic process and negotiate a compromise, putting on the table what they want, putting on the table what we want, and extricating what is mutually advantageous to us both so we can live together in harmony and coexist. See, I am not afraid to say what my position is. So for me, the same ennobling qualities that I brought to the table that allowed a Buster Douglas to have an opportunity to fight for the championship is the same qualities that I exemplify now.

When Buster Douglas became champion he has an obligation also; first of all, morally, spiritually, and then at the end of the trade, contractually. I supported him; I made a business investment. It's the same as anyone that would come in and commandeer your property after you'd paid for it—to take anything that you have from you—a right. And the right of the government is to protect its citizens' rights. That's all I'm asking. I didn't sue Buster. I can show you how ludicrous this is. I was arguing with Buster because Buster's feelings were hurt. But hurting people's feelings don't breach contracts. You understand? If I hurt your feelings, I apologize for that. But that don't breach a contract. I've done everything I'm supposed to do. I gave it my time, my effort, my finance. I gave it my ingenuity, my ability to go out and do things that I've been doing 18 years as the number-one promoter in the world. And then, at the end of the day because I hurt your feelings, the whole nine years goes down, with all that I subsidized you for the last five years; and you're going to say that's a reason for you not to talk to me? I talked to him when he disappointed me. It hurt me when he was fighting Tony Tucker when I just knew Buster was going to be the champion of the world. He walks up to me after the knockout and says, "I let you down. I didn't do what I was supposed to do." I said, "Well, Buster, since you recognize that, I forgive you. Now let's rededicate yourself to redouble your efforts, and let's go back and get him."

Member of the press: Is he willing to do that? Has he said he's going to sit down with you and talk?

Don King: Yes, he did. He *said* he did. I'm looking forward to him doing that, and I'm very happy and very appreciative and anticipating. Hopefully, I can do that today.

Member of the press: Since your contract is binding and valid, why not let the court agree with you and get this over with?

Don King: For one thing, why should we have to go there? The court wasn't there when I made the deal. The court wasn't there when I supported Buster Douglas. The court wasn't there when I carried Buster Douglas through the defeat to bring him back to victory.

Member of the press: And Steve Wynn?

Don King: Let me tell you about Steve Wynn. We talked about having the Tyson-Douglas fight in Vegas. He didn't want to go through with it after he talked to his people in the hotel. They said, "Don't bring that mismatch here." Steve Wynn showed how much he loved Buster and how much he wanted to be with him. After the fight in Japan he says I'm gonna supply Buster with lawyers and I'm gonna pay the lawyers. Then last Friday he dropped everything on John Johnson. He says, "the Mirage has no obligation to Buster Douglas. They came and asked me [Wynn] for an offer; I just merely made an offer 'cause they prevailed upon me. I have no interest in Buster

Douglas. I don't want be involved in this thing here. I'm just a hotel casino trying to have a fight."

Not true! He's a liar, a liar, unmitigated liar! Nevertheless, this shows you what he'd swear to under oath, which we're going to give to Mr. Johnson and his attorney. I'm not into this for no court battle. What they are trying to do is to separate the legacy that I'm very proud of, and no one can take that away. It's irrefutable and incontrovertible that I have, for the last 18 years, made more millionaires boxing—black and Hispanic—than have ever been known to mankind. So now, you can't take that away. To every one of them, my commitment has been loyalty, integrity, commitment, and it has been fulfilled. So they have all had second chances, from Muhammad Ali to Mike Tyson. Now Mike Tyson was the only way that I could've given Buster Douglas another opportunity to fight for the championship. So Mike asks me before the fight, "How's Buster?" I say, "He's a nice guy. He's a great challenge. Go out there and, if anything happens, Buster will naturally be doing the same thing you're doing." But Buster didn't prove to do that . Not because Buster knows better or don't know better, but because Buster's been misled.

I understand that reciprocity is the name of the game. I'm not fighting any kind of war, and most certainly I'm not going to let people use me as an instrument of racial divisiveness. You understand? You must understand that I'm a promoter of friendship, unanimity, and zeal bringing the races together. No one has ever heard me even knock America. We do know that we have a lot of inequities here in America for people of color. We do know that we have double or triple standards for people of color. But you got to fight to change the attitude. The laws change behavior. You can only change attitudes when you work in the vineyard; when you demonstrate that you can be successful in spite of the insurmountable barriers and difficulties.

Member of the press: Is today a political move, using the church for this press conference, asking Buster Douglas to come to the altar instead of to court?

Don King: No, I didn't even know you were going to be here. But when I saw the first girl outside the church and they asked me, "Why are you coming to church?" I mean, that in itself is a question that is ludicrous. You come to church to worship God. That's what I came to do, to get a spiritual refillment. In so doing I'm energized because I do believe in God. God says in His holy word that He and I are a majority. If I have faith in Him, then I can put my troubles aside, so I put my hands in God's hands. He said "I'll prepare a table before you in the presence of your enemies."

We must move out of the way of danger and keep moving in a positive manner. Actually, I'm gonna call John Johnson. I'm gonna call him directly and not let others intervene and cause a confusing situation. It's a very simple thing here. I want to protect my rights. I think I've earned that right. I think that you have to recognize that I've earned the right. Because what you're seeing is, Don King's not on trial here. American contract law is on trial. It's really immaterial to me. It will be interesting to see what's happened. I could lose an economic boon, but what the country would lose is inviolate. Once contract law is no good for me, it ain't no good for you. So it's thrown back into chaos.

Member of the press: How much money do you stand to lose if the courts rule in Buster's favor?

Don King: It's not how much money I stand to lose if the courts go in Buster's favor, it's how much *you* would lose. I think I could still make it. But if you find out that everything you're agreeing to and write down on paper under the auspices of the Constitution of these great United States is worthless, I think you are gonna be the big losers. This is what this is all about, and it's serious business. I didn't do anything wrong to Buster Douglas. An indiscretion may have happened; I have apologized for that because we all fall short of the mark and we all make human errors. I understand that, when people's feelings are hurt, you must strategize and do anything you can to placate and assuage them. I'm trying to do that.

I'm not here to fight with Johnson or Buster, and I'm not here to try to separate the two. But John Johnson must take this. When you start telling people to disavow their moral, spiritual, and contractual agreement, it can become too easy, because people who are inclined more to invective and accusation rather than speaking on their own behalves, so I have to do so with moderation. But when you start to tell people to disavow their contracts and their commitment when they haven't been breached—for the grace of God go me. If Buster were to wake up tomorrow and say, I've decided we ought to give Don King his rightful contribution out of this—they ain't giving me anything, you understand what I'm saying? I earn mine by promotions. I don't get one penny out of Buster's purse. Buster could get the same $20 million from me that he would get from Steve Wynn. Steve Wynn has just met Buster, refused him in 1990—and has never given him a dime to date. I have given Buster close to $3 million in his career. But my time and effort over this period of years is priceless because I have taken him to the championship. In fact, I got him there even earlier than the contract that was drawn said. Now, if Buster woke up in the morning and had a change of heart for whatever reason and says, "Well, now that we've gotten rid of King, that means there's more money in my pocket. What about me getting rid of Johnson? If I get rid of Johnson, since contracts don't mean anything, it would be another 25% that'd go into my pocket. I'm the champion of the world—I'd get it all myself."

Member of the press: You're saying that John Johnson is telling Buster Douglas to disavow his contract with you?

Don King: I think you've got that on film all over the country. You don't even have to ask me that question because this is what boggles my mind. Out of this whole thing, no one [has] ever seen me or heard me knock John Johnson and call him names like John is doing [to] me because I have taken the high side of it. I'm not in this for name-calling; this is business. This is strictly business. While I have a commitment and a mandate to the fighters that I promote, it is business with me. I'm in this for making me some money. I can make money. This is the secret. It's not hard for anyone else to know. . . . I can make money and at the same time, in the process of making money, help my people to elevate them[selves] to a better status of life, and teach them that it can be done in America in spite of the racism, the segregation, the bigotry, the biasness, and discrimination that has been in existence and that exists today, that we can change this by producing and performing. I'm not one of those that throw bricks through windows or Molotov cocktails that tear down buildings. I build buildings, I build relationships, I uplift people, not smash them. I mean black and white people alike, because we got to be here. It's a foregone conclusion that we're gonna have white people here and were gonna have black people here. So why should we go through the bickering and trying to degrade and disparage one another when we could work together in unity, friendship, and togetherness and make things happen that will be positive and constructive rather than destructive and detrimental. What I'm saying is that my obligation and my duty is to my people, the same as it would be for you to your people. And if out of this thing you bring a union of love and understanding, then each one of us respects one another.

Member of the press: Any last comments?

Don King: I most certainly don't want anyone in Columbus, because I am a black man, to think that I am anti-white in any way or that I would use that as an instigating bone of contention. That is not it; this is strictly business. This is a business obligation that Buster owes me. He don't have to like me now. We can both go to our respective base. I'll do my job; he can do his. If he don't want to speak to me in the interim of what we are doing, so be it. I'll do the best I can in promoting my event. But this is my living. And no one is supposed to be able to infringe upon your constitutional right to make a living. That's what this is all about. That's what makes America so great. I'm not interested in trying to degrade or deride Buster or John. I'm just trying to protect my God-given rights and my constitutional rights as an American. I am a first-class citizen of this great nation. It's about rights. And here we have a carpetbagger and a claim-jumper that would come in like a Steve Wynn that tried to come in through the back door and really confuse the situation. And torturously interfere with my contract, encouraging John Johnson to abort and to abrogate that contract and that commitment that he has.

Yesterday at the press conference Buster Douglas said I fulfilled my contract. He said that I put him on the fights, I did everything I was supposed to do, that I was a great man and that we would talk.

John Johnson said, "I like Don King, I always like to see him, he's always been there for us until he didn't recognize us." So now, if not recognizing in their perception—which I asked for forgiveness—is that an unpardonable sin that condemns to death? I'm just asking; that's all I want to know. I forgave them. John Johnson made to me many assurances about what Buster would do and what Buster would be and all these different things. He didn't live up to it. But I don't condemn John Johnson to the guillotine because Buster didn't keep his word and John Johnson didn't keep his word. I understood that John was involved emotionally and he wanted to help Buster. That was the overriding factor: I had an opportunity to help this man who was helping another man that was brought to me by his father, Billy Douglas. All right, so this goes on all the time. You can't get mad at them about these types of indiscretions. You must be able to understand, and that's all I'm asking them to do, to be as commiserate with my plight and as understanding with me as I am with them. That's all.

Member of the press: How long do you expect to be here?

Don King: I'm going to probably leave tomorrow because I'm optimistic that Mr. Douglas, Mr. Johnson, and I will meet today. I think that we should meet in the same spirit of brotherhood that we did when he came to me five years ago—and that I continued to maintain for five years without any questions when nobody knew who Buster was, probably not even you. It was Don King that was there. Always remember that the favor is in the extension, not in the pay back. That's an obligation and a duty. If I loan you money, that's the favor. But the time you pay it back, that's your obligation and duty. Sometimes people take it out of context and they mix their priorities. "Well, I paid you back, didn't I?" And when they say, "I paid you back," it's as though they've done you a favor. You have extended them a favor, and they're returning by paying the obligation. This is what I've done. I have extended the hand of fellowship to Buster Douglas and to John Johnson. I'm extending the olive branch now. So in this way, let us come in the same peace.

❏ ❑ ❐

John Johnson would attempt to counter the King offensive by calling his own press conference. John Johnson had achieved what few men can even dream. He achieved for himself and he was the driving force behind the man who reached the summit in his own profession, the world heavyweight champion, Buster Douglas. But Johnson could not be expected to match the master himself, Don King.

Douglas and Johnson, along with their entire championship boxing team, sat in stern solidarity in front of the Columbus press corps. Don King was among the audience that included Buster's father (sitting right behind King). What Johnson didn't know was even though it was Columbus, Ohio, they were playing on Don King's turf. It may have *seemed* that Johnson and Douglas would be able to control the message that day in Columbus, but in reality King had always worked the press like no other modern public personality. It didn't matter what city King operated in, he hadn't survived in this cutthroat business for 20 years without understanding and manipulating the power of the press. Johnson and Douglas didn't see it coming. They were in Don King's gun sight; it was like shooting fish in a barrel. By the end of the press conference it had become clear that a settlement between the parties was inevitable. Don King, in his own prophetic words, wasn't going to be left out of the carving of this turkey.

26

LARRY MERCHANT

*. . . which reminds us with savage eloquence that, if there's
a skinny man trying to get out of every fat man, there's also
a hero trying to get out of every ordinary man.*

—Larry Merchant

A week after the bout that would change both of their lives
in ways neither yet could possibly comprehend, James "Buster"
Douglas and "Iron" Mike Tyson squared off in close quarters once
more. This time the setting was a television studio, and boxing
commentator extraordinaire Larry Merchant served as referee. It
turned out that Merchant, a savvy and probing but evenhanded
inquisitor, had in mind landing a few necessary shots of his own.
The heaviest swings were saved for the dethroned champion and
for promoter Don King, absent but the acknowledged Richelieu
behind the heavyweight throne. Tyson ducked and counterpunched
against Merchant's verbal jabbing with more craftiness, if not
with particularly better results, than he had shown while crouch-
ing on the canvas inside the Tokyo Dome. Douglas, with savage
glory at his back and visions of conquest ahead, played it straight,
smooth, and sincere as if he really were, as Merchant character-
ized him, the newly anointed slayer of dragons.

The two fighters not so gallantly shook hands at Merchant's
urging. Neither appeared enthused about the required ritual, so
the exchange was forced and perfunctory, like that of two neighbor kids compelled by their parents to make up after a nasty spat.
As Merchant proceeded to pump the champion and the once-
champ, Douglas and Tyson, for the most part, hardly acknowledged

175

each other's presence. Both were lost in a land of their own dreams, a country that since a week ago had become strange and unfamiliar. The journeyman with masterful skills, who until now had not enough to show for them, had become the instant hero of everyman by routing, in a Manichean battle, not only the beast, but also by vanquishing the beast inside the beast. Tyson could not know that Buster Douglas, by the simple act of planting doubt, had wounded beyond complete healing the relentless and cold-blooded predator within that drove him and inspired so much terror in opponents that many were beaten before they stepped into the ring. Nor could Douglas know that too soon he would revert to mediocre form and as a result would have to face a sad truth: while the meek might inherit the earth, they cannot for long possess it.

Even the prescient Larry Merchant could not guess he was dealing with two youthful warriors on whose best day in boxing the sun had set. How could anyone, based on the past, imagine such a future? At the same time, how could anyone be certain the sun would rise again after what had transpired on a recent winter afternoon in Japan? Merchant looked into the television camera and pronounced that he remained unbelieving. "Hi, I'm Larry Merchant," he told the electronic audience, "still willing to bet that Tyson would beat Douglas last week."

But something, he allowed, had gone askew in the natural order. Fairy tales no longer counted as fiction. Hack Hollywood scripts, the kind that make a stock storybook caricature like Rocky Balboa into a metaphor for the ultimate triumph of both a defeated America and a fading American dream, had grown flesh and blood and sinew. The flesh and blood had a name and a birth certificate. The name grew up not in a tarnished, self-doubting, Old Guard town like Philadelphia—or, for that matter, Brooklyn—but in its Midwest antithesis—buttoned-down, prosperous, sprawling, and self-satisfied Columbus, Ohio. The name was Buster Douglas. Or so a media-stoked hero's tale had been suggesting, not the least subtly, for the past week.

The story's climax had passed, but the denouement had proved needlessly messy. There had been controversy inspired, it was suspected, by Don King's desire to keep the Gaming House of Tyson, where King never before had lost a bet, from being forced to declare a holiday while it got the books back in order. In King's experience, Tyson in the ring was a slot machine that paid on every pull of the lever, and in the promoter's cunning estimation the house jackpot could be assured only if Evander Holyfield's name was matched with Tyson's when the spinning stopped. From Tyson's rudimentary perspective, Douglas simply, although surprisingly, had taken his title. To King, Douglas had not only usurped a boxing crown, he had shaken worlds, shattered scenarios, and obliterated plans.

Whether the result of a fluke or not, the previous week's anticipated walkover fighter had taken what didn't belong to him and, in doing so, had become the supreme force to be reckoned with, the possibility of which could not be found in any plot Machiavelli had worked out. Almost immediately after Tyson's thunderous fall King had decried the result, charging that a long count by referee Octavio Meyran had saved Douglas from a fight-ending KO after a Tyson uppercut had floored the challenger at the end of the eighth round. If Meyran had been doing his job, King asserted, the ignominious final two rounds would never have happened. Before his man even had been counted out, King had chased down Jose Sulaiman of the WBC to vent his professed belief that Tyson was being cheated out of a knockout victory. And in the disorderly hours in Tokyo after Tyson's loss, King, the ex-con from Cleveland who'd grown an empire, announced to the world that "everybody has seen the facts, and the facts are irrefutable and incontrovertible."

King demanded that the World Boxing Council and the World Boxing Association withhold their sanctioning of the Douglas victory. And for about as long as a spoiled child can hold its breath both commissions did as King commanded, a testimony to the power of a calculated tantrum tossed by the wielder of the purse. Demonstrating as much shameless brazenness as that of a world-class grifter, King the shaman was trying to do outside the boxing ring what Tyson the mauler could not do inside the ring in Japan—

that is, to keep his solitary grasp on the undisputed and unified heavyweight championship of the world. King's display, though, seemed strange and even counterproductive in one important sense: he promoted Douglas's fights as well as Tyson's. Still, his relationship with each fighter was vastly different. The infinitely ambitious and self-serving King had his lock on Tyson's career; John Johnson, who appeared to desire only what was best for his man, guided Douglas. If the crown had been passed, King no longer controlled the keys of the kingdom. Suddenly cast outside the gated wall, he was almost desperate when he raucously tried to storm back inside.

King did not make noise for long. The public and with almost no exception the media took the upstart's side. They quickly saw, as Merchant pointed out during the telecast, King and Tyson "as losers looking for alibis." Under immense pressure from virtually all corners, the boxing authorities decided that Douglas had won the title. Still, the controversy and the delay in declaring his victory legitimate had drained Douglas's triumph of some of its promised sweetness. As for King, by the time he got back to New York he was rewriting his own recent history. "There's never been a question from our side as to who the heavyweight champion of the world was," King told the assembled at a news conference.

At King's side, Tyson conceded to reality, asserting now that a boxing title should be won and lost in the ring and not in some smoke-filled, wood-paneled office with seconds, lawyers, agents, and promoters doing the fighting. However, saying he was not discouraged, Tyson all but pleaded for an immediate shot at vindication after his lone defeat in 38 professional bouts. "I'm just saying Mike's not going off the deep end," he declared in what can be viewed today as an amalgam of premonition and psychological denial. "The only thing I ask for is a rematch, then I'll take care of everything from there. That's all I'm asking for—the chance." He and King had, after all, given Douglas a chance. Next time, though, Douglas would have to fight the "real" Mike Tyson, the intimidator who for reasons that could only be guessed did not show up in Tokyo.

In the television studio, Merchant seemed far less fixated on the fallen champ's future prospects than he was on the opportunity so recently, so unexpectedly, and seemingly so casually tossed away. In a preamble to the interviews, Merchant declared that while boxing as sport is capable of being raised to transcendence through the courage and skill displayed by combatants inside the ring, it too often sinks into base injustice and crass exploitation perpetrated by the moneychangers outside of it. Noting that this time justice ultimately had prevailed, Merchant wryly observed that such an outcome in the boxing world should itself be considered an upset. Douglas, he granted, had shaken and reassembled the current paradigm when it came to champ and challengers, much as Muhammad Ali had done almost a generation earlier when, still as brash Cassius Clay, he had toppled the seemingly invincible Sonny "The Bear" Liston. Reaching for a dramatic comparison with what Douglas had accomplished in Tokyo, Merchant recounted a scene in 1964 in Miami when he had witnessed Clay standing inside the ropes and shouting to iconic and soon-to-be-dead singer Sam Cooke at ringside, "Sam, did I shock the world?"

That had happened long ago. The temblors of Tokyo had not yet subsided. Tyson had shocked in the way Liston had shocked, by losing a fight almost no one thought he could lose. The odds makers first had installed Tyson as a 42-1 favorite, and the play of the smart money had become so one-sided the fight finally was taken off the board in Las Vegas. In Merchant's estimation of what had spectacularly come to pass, Tyson had not unleashed as much thunder during the fight as he had in the hours after his crown had been taken and his reputation as the planet's most fearsome fighter diminished. Merchant addressed an incredibly shrunken man when he questioned why Tyson had collaborated, if only briefly, with King to further diminish himself by trying to deny Douglas the title based on a supposed long count. He asked about the outburst immediately after the fight during which Tyson had declared himself still the champion and in the days after which, when facing a public outcry, Tyson had recanted, saying instead that all he really wanted was a rematch. Merchant sharply pressed the issue, wondering aloud what this day's "spin" was going to be.

Tyson, ever the aggressor in the ring, appeared to cover up against Merchant's provocative probing. Countering the first sharp query, Tyson pointed out that he had not filed a protest, mouthing a technical truth. The response, at the same time, evaded the troubling question of whether the public griping about the eighth-round knockdown of Douglas had been a trial balloon to test exactly the limits of King's expansive power with the boxing organizations that fed well at the table King set for them. No, Tyson insisted now, he didn't think that anyone but Buster Douglas deserved the title, an assertion he would repeat several times during the broadcast. Tyson did not outright deny either that in Tokyo he had questioned the count or that he had stated the decision was unfair and so still considered himself the heavyweight champion. This day, however, he was not ready to go quite so far as to outrage a television audience that knew better. "How many things in boxing are fair?" he said to Merchant, who had an answer but remained silent as Tyson continued. "I had 37 good nights. But, then again, the reason I call myself champ is because I still consider myself the best fighter in the world."

Merchant wasn't about to let Tyson escape with merely shadowboxing around the truth. He wanted details about what had led up to the long-count brouhaha. What were Tyson's thoughts immediately after the bout? How had he come to believe he'd been the victim of a long count? In answer to those queries, Tyson initially remarked that he began to ask himself questions about the count as soon as he reached the dressing room. However, he was spurred into taking his questions public, he said, only when observers, including ring officials from Japan and from the WBA and WBC, began to clamor about what had unfolded during the eighth round. The fact that nothing eventually became of all that sound and fury, Tyson claimed, really was no big deal to him. "Nobody is crying over spilled milk," he told Merchant before turning toward his conqueror. "Buster, people believe you're the champion of the world. We'll do it again."

Douglas did not rise to either piece of bait that dangled in Tyson's comment. As for the suggestion of a rematch, he let his manager Johnson make bouts. Insofar as the title, he at last possessed the belts that dubbed him heavyweight champion regardless of what Tyson, King, or the world believed. Merchant, though, wanted to know what effect, if any, the post-fight controversy had on him. Douglas responded that initially he did not know about the protest but in short order learned about it from Johnson. He told Merchant he had difficulty grasping what his manager told him, let alone understanding flimsy justifications that led to a seemingly pointless controversy. Douglas had won the fight by flooring an unbeaten heavyweight who had never before viewed a ring from canvas level. In the momentary mix of astonishment and glorious triumph after the knockout, neither Douglas nor Johnson had foreseen a flight back to Columbus without two of championship belts that they, and most of the watching world, thought clearly belonged to them. Yes, Douglas told Merchant, he was disappointed the WBA and WBC had held up his claim, made irrefutably in the ring, to the title. Yes, the controversy had taken something important away from what should have been an ascendant boxing star's most thrilling and exultant moment. The feeling, Douglas said, was as if something had been left undone. He had reached the height, but validation of that accomplishment was not forthcoming. "I still felt that I won the fight," he told Merchant. "It was just that it wasn't completed. Being completed was receiving both belts."

And as to the cooked-up matter of why he had not immediately received those belts? Douglas's recall of the eighth round included a knockdown but not a knockout somehow missed by the referee. "I was up before the count of 10," he told Merchant. "They were saying it was a long count, but to my knowledge it was six. I picked it up at six." Of course, the King-Tyson camp had contended that the six should have been a 10 because Meyran, the referee, had wasted seconds after Douglas went down before he began the count. The fight, therefore, should have been over. Merchant was preparing to refute that interpretation of what had

transpired, but first he wanted Douglas's recollection of the knockdown. The champ, insisting the punch had not hurt him, said Tyson
had caught him off-balance and leaning. Thus, he had fallen backward the result more of happenstance, like a baseball batter sent
to the seat of his pants by the graze of a brush-back pitch, than
because of a devastating blow.

As proof of his clear-headed state, Douglas reminded Merchant and Tyson that he had slammed the canvas in disgust after
his silly blunder, a blunder he attributed to a lapse in focus in-
duced by a flush of misplaced overconfidence. Not only had he
survived farther into the fight than all but a few could have foreseen, Douglas sensed that he actually was winning. Just as he had
begun to allow himself to get comfortable with his dominance,
he had paid for that spell of big-headedness by getting knocked
down. "I got up on strong legs," Douglas said to Merchant, and
he maintained he could have stood upright sooner if the count
had required that he do so. All the same, the bell ending the round
almost immediately sounded, denying Tyson an opportunity to
press what appeared to be an advantage he had announced with a
lightning jolt. Douglas, given time to compose himself between
rounds, came out in the ninth lucid with purpose and aware of
what his hubristic blunder had almost cost him. Armed with a
determination that there would be no more mistakes, he immediately began to regain control. The decisive 10th ended early with
the shocking sight of Tyson on all fours fumbling for his lost
mouthpiece as Meyran counted him out. It was over. Or so Douglas and Johnson had every reason to believe.

Such, too, was Merchant's conclusion. In unblinking hindsight aided by replay, the television host showed Tyson, Douglas,
viewers, and King, if he cared to watch, that the supposedly long,
14-second count by referee Octavio Meyran in fact had not been
unusually long at all. With tape of the disputed knockdown rolling, Merchant made four points, all of them visual refutations of
King's post-fight claim and all of which became obvious to anyone watching. First, he said as video backed his words, Meyran
began his count two seconds after the timekeeper had began, a

discrepancy, to be sure, but not one that deserved to have altered the outcome. By rule, the referee and not the timekeeper controls the count, and Meyran, by the standards of most fights, had shown no hesitation to take charge of his duty. Second, Douglas's actions while on the canvas clearly demonstrated that he was not in the throes of near-unconsciousness and could have stood on his feet sooner, as he contended, had the count required him to do so. Third, the timekeeper in actuality had erred by starting his count the instant Douglas hit the canvas, whereas one second should have elapsed before the count of one. Finally, in a bit of perhaps serendipitous coincidence that made confetti out of King's claim, the elapsed time from the moment in the 10th round when Tyson hit the canvas until he was counted out amounted precisely to 14 seconds. "So it's pretty well established," Merchant observed, "that the 10-count took 14 seconds to implement for both fighters."

Later in the broadcast, Merchant bolstered his point by showing film of arguably boxing's most famous "long count," after which Gene Tunney, on Sept. 22, 1927, got up from a knockdown at Soldier's Field in Chicago to defeat Jack Dempsey by decision for the heavyweight title. The footage showed Tunney had not been saved by the count, a fact Dempsey acknowledged in an accompanying film clip shot a few years after his loss. Implying that King and Tyson ought especially to take heed, Merchant offered his verdict: "The 14-second knockout is commonplace." With those words, Octavio Meyran was absolved of error, of incompetence, and of any wrongdoing.

In pursuing his suspicion that Tyson's post-fight tirade had been a spurious concoction, Merchant asked Tyson whether at the close of the eighth round—in real time, in other words—he had any notion Douglas had benefited from a long count. Tyson's answer was not precisely the same one he had given earlier in the interview, when he recalled not considering the possibility of a long count until he had returned to the dressing room. Now Tyson remembered he had heard "somebody," possibly a cornerman, say the fight was over as he stood watching Meyran make the count. The materializing realization that he appeared to have won,

Tyson said, explained why at that point he began jumping trium-
phantly in what turned out to be a brief and premature celebration. Merchant never asked whether Tyson might have misinterpreted
his corner's comments, although such could have been the case.
A declaration by someone in his corner that "it's over," if it happened at all, could have meant Tyson had won, but it also could
have been nothing more than a case of a partisan's wishful thinking uttered out loud.

Tyson, at any rate, backpedaled on the question of whether
he thought at that moment Douglas should have been counted
out. "I know these things happen," he said, "and I'm in the wrong
position to complain, because regardless if it was a long count or
not, regardless, those things happen." Tyson acknowledged he
had been made aware as the fight progressed into the middle
rounds that he might be in trouble on points, but he figured it was
only a matter of time before he could reach Douglas with a toxic
shot that would make the judges' scorecards superfluous. Tyson
was not blaming anyone but himself for Douglas's survival but,
he said, had the bell not sounded after the eighth-round knockdown he might have ended it right there. No, he insisted once
more in answer to a Merchant question, he had not been embar-
rassed by King's attempt to finagle for him a victory demonstra-
bly undeserved. Tyson termed as "ludicrous" Merchant's
suggestion that perhaps, unlike many of his predecessors—champions like Dempsey and Ali who had shown grace in defeat—
"Iron" Mike had demonstrated during the post-fight episode that
he could not handle getting beat. "I've dealt with defeats all my
life," Tyson countered. "Those things happen."

Nonetheless, not many observers, probably Tyson and King
least of all, thought Tokyo would unravel as it did. The world did
not hold sufficient imagination, except among a few fantasists, to
foresee an unbeaten champion's defeat in that time, in that place,
and particularly against that opponent. While throughout his carefully constructed and heretofore modestly successful career, Douglas had demonstrated vulnerability at unexpected times. Tyson,
on the other hand, had marched through recent opponents with

the merciless ferocity of Genghis Khan sweeping across the Eurasian steppes. Conquering every comer, Tyson arrived not long out of his teens as the youngest heavyweight champion ever on Nov. 22, 1986, when he battered Trevor Berbick into a two-round TKO to take the WBC crown. Four months later, he claimed the WBA title by winning a 12-round unanimous decision against James "Bonecrusher" Smith.

From that point until Tokyo, Tyson neither made it a practice nor built his fear-provoking reputation by craftily out-pointing opponents; typically, he brutalized them. During his championship years covering a run of eight unified title fights, any outcome for a challenger other than a KO or a TKO in a Tyson brawl had become a rarity. Rarely did an opponent last 12 rounds. In the bout before Douglas, Tyson had taken out Carl "The Truth" Williams in 93 seconds. Two fights previous, Frank Bruno had gone down in the first before getting up to absorb a five-round pummeling and a TKO. Michael Spinks, who had come into a hyped showdown of unbeatens with a record of 31-0, lasted 91 seconds. Tony Tubbs survived but two rounds, Larry Holmes four, and Tyrrell Biggs seven. What seemed even more startling was that at age 24, most ring experts agreed, Tyson had yet to reach his athletic prime. After Tokyo, with his aura of invincibility reduced to the status of a shadowy myth exposed, Tyson was forced to confront doubts he had never before experienced.

Merchant, circling over the freshly fallen, swooped in to pick a few bones. Pressed by Merchant about the knockout, Tyson said his swelling eye, tortured in the late rounds by Douglas's jabs, and the sometimes-close infighting at the end kept him from seeing the right hand that rocked him off his feet and into the ranks of ex-champions. The punch had not knocked him senseless, Tyson said. As proof, he pointed to his attempt to locate and replace the mouthpiece. Many observers, however, had interpreted that vivid and pathetic scene as a pitiable symbol of a great boxer's astonishing and sudden downfall. What Tyson left unacknowledged was the simple truth that the mouthpiece had been sent flying, along with Tyson's sweat and blood, by a force that flesh, bone, and brain are not designed to withstand. To his credit, Tyson never called the deciding punch lucky. And although he had suggested in earlier statements he might not have been at his best in Tokyo, Tyson hedged when responding to Merchant's probing about possible overconfidence and to questions about both his physical and mental preparation. "Regardless of the situation as to why I wasn't fighting well," Tyson said, "you can't take from the fact that Buster won the championship."

At times Merchant badgered. He questioned the lack of experience by Tyson's cornermen. It was they, he suggested, who had failed between rounds to work properly on the battered and closing left eye that left their man vulnerable to the increasingly invisible missiles fired from Douglas's right hand. It was they, Merchant asserted, who had not forced on Tyson the discipline to prepare for Douglas. It was Tyson's misplaced allegiance to old friends, Merchant proposed, that prevented him from bringing in a master who could set straight Tyson's errant and increasingly undisciplined ways both inside and outside the ring. For his part, Merchant was groping for an explanation of what must have appeared to him, as it did to others, as unexplainable. Tyson, in response, accused Merchant of insulting his intelligence, of a "ridiculous" misrepresentation about his handlers, of misconstruing what happened in those final rounds. "We went out there and lost to the guy that fought the best that night," Tyson said, signaling his acceptance of the finality of the outcome. The truth is, Merchant's interview revealed a fighter having difficulty not so much with a mouthpiece but with facing the fact that in myriad ways he had not shown his best before, during, or immediately after a fight from which he would never find the inner resources to fully redeem himself.

During his exchanges with Merchant, Douglas, too, proved at least once contradictory, although probably not as the result of guile. Merchant, challenging Douglas's post-fight assertion that he had defeated Tyson "on instinct," wondered about a game plan. Douglas granted that he had entered the ring with a plan, and that plan was to use "speed and lateral movement." The idea, which the 6-foot-4 Douglas executed with a precision he had not always executed fight plans in the past and would never do so again, was to keep the 5-foot-11 Tyson, with his much shorter reach, from boring inside, especially early, where the combination of a street brawler's strength and infighting skills were incomparable and inevitably lethal.

For reasons he could not adequately explain but perhaps having to do with the recent death of his mother and the influence of Johnson, Douglas entered the ring in Tokyo without the onerous baggage of fear brought to their bouts with Tyson by the likes of Spinks, Smith, and others, particularly the recent opponents. Johnson had managed to show Douglas that Tyson had as many flaws as a fighter as he seemed to have as a man. As his confidence had grown into hubris over the years, Tyson began to abandon both the boxing and life lessons his trainer, the late Cus D'Amato, had tried to instill in him. Tyson the champ not only had become distracted outside the ring, but inside he had become less of craftsman and more of a puncher dependent on knocking out opponents mesmerized beyond hope of victory.

Johnson told Douglas such a fighter was not, as he might appear to be, invincible. Further, an opponent who is able to stay out of harm's way by countering and jabbing as long as it takes to outbox such a fighter or to find a decisive opening, need not fear him, Johnson counseled. Johnson presented the plan; he then somehow convinced Douglas the plan would work. No doubt everything that Johnson had told him still was running through Douglas's head, but it never came out of his mouth when Merchant asked how Douglas had managed his emotions against a force that had terrorized so many others. He offered the simple answer of a warrior, the answer that must go back beyond the gladiatorial arenas to an even earlier time when men roamed the earth in tribes and fought each other to the death not for entertainment and purses but for dominance. "I'm a man and he's a man also," Douglas said, "and I accepted the challenge." Douglas maintained that in Tokyo he had not seen a Tyson any different than his usual assassin self, which some people cited as the reason for the "impossible" upset.. Tyson had not stopped advancing throughout the bout. He had kept fighting, no differently from 37 previous fights. Nonetheless, Douglas, except for those anomalous moments at the end of Round 8, felt in control. It was the plan at work.

No less an authority than consummate cornerman Angelo Dundee, whose long partnership with Muhammad Ali and Sugar Ray Leonard had made him a legend, gave Johnson credit for engineering Tyson's downfall. One of the few ring tacticians publicly willing to say before the fight that Douglas had a chance against Tyson, Dundee told Merchant that his reason for doing so had as much to do with Johnson's motivational and tactical skills as with the physical attributes Douglas could muster against the shorter Tyson. Dundee said he had co-managed a fighter with Johnson, Steve Gregory, and he knew from that experience Douglas had "the right guy behind him." Dundee wasn't reluctant to say that he knew Johnson could draw something out of Douglas that others could not. Douglas himself backed up Dundee's assessment, telling Merchant, "I fought at the best of my capabilities." For that, Douglas could take credit. But, as Dundee asserted, he had to give Johnson credit, too.

Contrarily, Tyson's co-trainers, Aaron Snowell and Jay Bright, took a public pounding both for not having their man ready and for their handling of the fight. Kevin Rooney, Tyson's fired ex-trainer, questioned his successors' competence, as did others. Setting aside questions about Tyson's conditioning and mental preparedness coming into Tokyo, the cornermen left themselves particularly vulnerable by their actions, or lack thereof, at ringside. First, the critics charged, they had failed to properly work on Tyson's swollen and closing eye. Second, they had showed themselves unable or unwilling to confront Tyson with the uneasy but growing recognition that he was heading for defeat with each passing round. Merchant added his own shot, reminding the audience of his fight night remark that "if you had a Secretariat, you don't put just any jockey on him—you get the best because even great athletes need help to get out of trouble—which Tyson definitely was in." The implication, of course, was that Tyson had not surrounded himself with people who could help him. Nobody in the Tyson camp, it seemed, had been able to imagine that a time might come when their champion would need help.

Merchant turned to Gil Clancy, a famed trainer before he became a CBS commentator, for his critique on Tyson's cornermen, and Clancy found egregious fault. The ice bag used to decrease swelling, Clancy said, had been improperly handled. To be effective, melted ice has to be continually replaced and the bag packed full, with a minimum of air and water. Tyson's corner, to Clancy's eyes, had failed Ice Bag 101, the most basic course in bruise control. Further, and more important, it appeared the corner in its deference and idol worship had been unable to muster the courage to arouse Tyson to the growing peril Douglas presented. Clancy recalled how Angelo Dundee had saved Sugar Ray Leonard in a welterweight title fight against Thomas "Hit Man" Hearns with a grating wakeup in which he famously told Leonard, "You're blowing the fight, son." Clancy recounted his own renowned rousing of a sluggish Emil Griffith with a physical slap that sent the astonished welterweight to a title. In Tokyo, Tyson had needed someone in his corner neither afraid nor awed nor beholden to tell him he was in trouble, Clancy said, and it seemed apparent that the cost of not having that presence was the title. Even more than that, though, by allowing the loss, Tyson and his handlers had forfeited the intangible that no other contemporary could overcome in a fight. "He always had a tremendous advantage with intimidation. . . . Nobody could beat him, 'Iron' Mike Tyson," Clancy said, almost scoffing. "I've always said he's not iron, but he's made out of flesh and blood." The next time, Clancy predicted, "the other guy is not going to have that much respect for him."

Whether the next time would be a rematch with Douglas or whether Tyson would have to wait for the outcome of a Douglas-Holyfield fight was, for the time being, a question without an answer. The controversy fostered by King and Tyson had been "bogus," out-and-out artifice that, now in the past, demanded little additional consideration, Douglas told Merchant. Back in Johnson's native West Virginia the boys would be laughing at the trumped-up controversy, saying it was plain all along that King's dog wouldn't hunt. Well, maybe not all along. At any rate, while the entire distasteful episode had been relegated to the past, residual hard feelings remained. The attempt to withhold the title planted anger and disappointment in the Douglas-Johnson camp, but whether lingering resentments would interfere with future business remained a matter for conjecture. King, bowing to public sentiment, the facts, and laying groundwork for the next big-money bout, had apologized. Douglas, seeing as no lasting harm had been done by the post-fight chicanery, accepted King's overture. Douglas's history with King, not to mention King's stature, gave the champ reason to look past indiscretions made by the game's prime mover. Douglas explained to Merchant that King always had been "upright" with him, putting him on championship undercards even after some weak performances. It was as if, perhaps rightly, Douglas felt he still owed King something. But what?

Tyson was campaigning unashamedly for an immediate rematch. Neither the defeat nor the loss of the title chafed as much as the way he, the self-proclaimed "best fighter in the world," had performed, Tyson told Merchant. It seemed clear Tyson was not asking merely for another shot at the title; he wanted immediate redemption. He reminded Merchant that he had fought Douglas even though Douglas had not been the No. 1 contender. Pointing toward his conqueror, Tyson suggested, "it would only be right for him to do the same" as a gesture of reciprocity. The No. 1 contender Holyfield, meanwhile, was stating publicly that he was preparing to fight Douglas, a position backed by Shelley Finkel, his manager, although no deal had yet been discussed. Douglas told Merchant he was willing to fight either Holyfield or Tyson, whatever match presented the best offer as determined by King and Johnson.

Amid all the speculation about what was in store for Douglas, Clancy and Dundee had offered their idea: Douglas likely would again handle Tyson if there were to be a rematch. However, Merchant, looking at a career that showed few previous signs of uninterrupted excellence, seemed less certain about anything involving Buster Douglas except the week-ago past when an apparent journeyman boxer had put himself on an unlikely pedestal. Had it been a beginning or an aberration? Merchant wondered whether Douglas, in his victory over Tyson, had not merely for one night found something within himself that almost no one knew resided there. He wondered whether, after having surprised the world, Douglas had discovered the indefinable something that lies beyond the grasp of mediocre man but which greatness takes for granted. Douglas said he could sustain what he had found. He was the champ and that would make the difference. He was his own hero now.

27

WHAT NEXT?

"I wish *I were Don King."*

—Donald Trump

A parallel in real life can be drawn from the ending of Sidney Pollack's great film, *The Candidate.* Robert Redford's character in the film had just pulled off an improbable political upset. His entire world had been focused on winning the election of his life. With the post-election celebration swirling around him, the newly elected United States Senator stood dazed, looking blankly at his political manager. Amid all the chaos he finally asks, "Now what do we do?"

Manager John Johnson's dream had come true. And not unlike his friend and new world champion, he was sitting on top of the boxing world. But now what was he going to do? All Johnson had were questions and he was alone in his new quest to find the answers. Should he give into the pressure of Don King and Mike Tyson and negotiate for the much-anticipated rematch, or should he look for another financial player and give the number-one challenger, Evander Holyfield, the title shot? Woody Hayes's old ghost would return again to help Johnson find his way. "When in doubt John, keep it simple, just run straight the hell at 'em," he could still hear Woody say. So John Johnson's final strategy for the next fight became as simple as it gets. "We'll fight for whoever pays us the most."

Enter Steve Wynn.

Steve Wynn doesn't like to lose. As a matter of fact, if you trace back his business life it would seem that every venture he touched turned to gold. Wynn, who grew up in New Haven, Connecticut, and whose father operated a string of bingo parlors and would eventually alter the very face of Las Vegas, now wanted to become a major player in the world of professional boxing. How hard could it be?

The phone call came from Bob Halloran, president of sports for the Mirage Resorts, calling on behalf of Steve Wynn. Buster and John Johnson had just returned to Columbus after the David Letterman taping. The phone calls were now streaming in from all over the world. One day Johnson received a call from a representative of Bahrain in the Middle East. The country wanted to host Buster's next fight and money would be no object. Although tempting, Johnson again was looking over his shoulder at his old conservative mentor Woody Hayes. The United States was in the middle of the first war in the Middle East and Johnson just couldn't bring himself to consider taking Buster to that region for the next fight. Not with Woody watching.

Bob Halloran flew to Columbus and met with Johnson at the Embassy Suites Hotel. Over dinner Halloran told Johnson that Steve Wynn, the largest casino owner in the world, wanted to expand into professional boxing and he wanted to start by promoting Buster's next fight at the Mirage. He offered to fly Johnson and Buster out to Vegas to meet directly with Wynn. At first Johnson refused the offer because he didn't want to lose control of the bidding process. He understood how seductive a trip on Wynn's private jet followed by wining and dining in the city of lights could be. No, he would first entertain all offers and if he decided on Wynn and the Mirage they would fly out after an agreement was reached. But Wynn personally called Johnson the next day and before the week was out both he and Buster were jetting out to the desert. Steve Wynn flew to Columbus with his friend Julius Erving ("Doctor J") to pick up Johnson and Buster.

The seduction had begun.

On the flight out to Las Vegas Johnson was feeling good. Here was the boy from the end of the road in West Virginia now flying above it all. "It felt safe up there," Johnson reflects back.

"For the first time in a long time I was feeling no pressure, it was like being in heaven." As he drifted off during the flight Johnson thought back to the not too distant past. He was back on the corner of Broad and High street in downtown Columbus with J. D. McCauley and Buster Douglas. They were watching a parade for Jerry Page who had just won a gold medal in boxing at the 1984 Summer Olympics. His eyes closed, Johnson could still see Page sitting in the car next to Columbus Mayor Buck Rinehart with that huge gold medal around his neck. The three of them stood silently as Page past them that day. "We didn't have five bucks in our pockets between us," Johnson smiles, shaking his head. "And here I am six years later, flying in a private jet owned by one of the richest men in the world about ready to talk to him about more money than I could even imagine. Only in America."

It was about to get even stranger. John Johnson was Alice in Wonderland. Wynn arranged for Buster and Johnson to stay in private bungalows at the Mirage. Steve Wynn's Las Vegas is not your typical wining and dining. Live volcanoes and live exotic animal acts welcomed the two boys from the Midwest. Johnson was getting calls in his bungalow from all parts of the country on behalf of Steve Wynn. And they all said the same thing: you could take his word to the bank. "Nothing that has happened between us, from the moment I stepped on that jet to this day, has proven those people wrong," Johnson says. "He may be the most brilliant man I've ever known, and he'll always be a special person in my life. He was a wonderful friend to me and I feel ashamed that we let him down."

There would be other people calling Johnson. "As soon as I heard the voice saying, 'Coach, congratulations, it was a great, great accomplishment, what you and Buster did,' I knew who it was. It was Bill Cosby. Cosby was appearing at the Hilton and he invited us to come over after his show and visit. It's a strange sensation when you spend time with someone you've seen on TV for most of your life. Cosby gave me his phone numbers when we left and said, 'If you ever need to reach me feel free to call.' He was very gracious and I can tell you his call meant a lot to James and to me. He told Buster as long as he listened to Coach J. J. things would go great."

But the call from Bill Cosby would seem insignificant compared to the call that followed. John Johnson is known for coining the following phrase, "the two men who've influenced me most in my life are Jesus Christ and Woody Hayes . . . and not necessarily in that order." But in truth the man who called Johnson next may trump the big two—Muhammad Ali. "It's hard for me to put into words how proud I am that Muhammad Ali would actually advise James that if he continued listening to his 'coach' he would achieve greatness. The noblest of men referring to me as a member of the noblest profession, it doesn't get any better than that."

Johnson had been in Wonderland for two days when all of sudden Don King appeared. "He came up and hugged me and told me how much he loved me right there in the Mirage lobby. We went immediately to my bungalow. It was a crowded place. King had several people with him, including his son Carl. Also hanging out in the bungalow was Tim May from the *Columbus Dispatch*, and Ian Thomsen from the *National Sports Daily*."

King went right for the jugular, "You can't deal me out John; this is where I make my bonanza!" When Don King gets rolling no amount of formal training or preparation could ever prepare you for his approach. Still glaring at Johnson he continued. "The sad thing is we've got this turkey sitting here ready to eat, and we can't slice it up." What King didn't know was it was too late for him, a deal was on the table. Johnson had already met with Wynn and agreed to $25 million for a fight at the Mirage against Evander Holyfield.

"You offered us $10 million, Don, and now James is getting $25 million. James is going to make more money than anybody has ever made in this business, and that's the way it should be. You're not taking it away from James," Johnson emotionally responded.

"He's not making more," King replied his voice getting louder. "He's making all of it! That's not the way it should be, there's enough money for everybody. Buster shouldn't make it all. You go from [earning] 50 thousand to 1.3 million [for Tyson], to 25 million, and he should keep all of it?"

Johnson smiled and enthusiastically nodded his head up and down.

"John, you're a stupid motherf—er!" King responded while slamming his fist on a table. "You're in way over your head. I'm going to come back and kick your ass!" King ranted.

"You can make your own deal with Wynn," Johnson responded. "But James Douglas is not taking any less money."

John Johnson talks passionately about his concern for Buster Douglas and those like him. "I was negotiating for James Buster Douglas. I wasn't negotiating for a fight, or for an event. I wasn't seeking revenge because of the way King treated us after the Tyson fight. This was about what is fair and just. James Douglas deserves the money, not me, and not Don King. The *fighter* is putting his ass on the line, not the promoter. The people are turning on their TVs to see the fighter, not the promoter. The arenas are filled because the people want to see the gladiators in the ring, not the people who hang out in $1,000-a-night bungalows and talk about 'carving up the turkey.' This is something I truly believe in. I'm happy that baseball players and football players are getting their fair share of the billions coming into their respective sport. I think it shows great progress that Oprah Winfrey is the producer of her TV show and not just getting paid a salary that some exec determines she deserves. *She's* the show, not some hack executive. It's about time that the individual is getting justly compensated in this country. I guess you could say as between labor and management, I'm a labor man."

Back in the bungalow King started playing the race card, turning to J. D. McCauley trying to divide McCauley and Johnson. Johnson couldn't take any more and called Wynn and told him to get King out of the bungalow.

When Wynn arrived, King attacked him immediately. "I'm going to own this fucking hotel," King screamed. "$600 million and I'm going to own it." Johnson smiles when he thinks back on

King's threat. "Not many people know this but we came close to owning Steve Wynn's hotel ourselves, well part of it anyway. Late in our negotiations, after I had asked for $30 million, and Wynn countered with the final $25 million offer, out of nowhere I recountered by asking for 200,000 shares of Mirage stock in addition to the $25 million. I'll never forget the look on Wynn's face as he glared at me and said, 'What the fuck happened to Woody Hayes?' He finally said okay to the shares but only on the condition that James would defeat Holyfield."

Deal done.

Wynn calmly picked up a chair, walked over, sat down right in front of King, and said, "Don, you're a no good, lying, thieving motherf—er. You're extinct."

Within weeks lawsuits were cross-filed. Douglas and Johnson sued King in Nevada to get out of their contract with King, and King sued Douglas and Wynn in New York to force Douglas to fight for him.

"It is something called 'torturous interference of a contract,'" Johnson reflects. "That's what they call the lawsuit that Don King filed against us. I'd never heard of such a thing. I offered King $3 million to simply walk away. He said he couldn't feed his family and support his staff on such a small figure. I honestly thought we could still work this out but in the end we all ended up in court."

The trial was in part a glimpse of the underworld of professional boxing. Johnson feared for his life during this period and ended up obtaining a license to carry a gun. He confesses to his legal naiveté. "I just assumed that whoever took the stand and told the truth the jury would see and rule correctly. I felt we had the truth on our side."

The trial in New York began on July 2, 1990. It was reality TV before we had reality TV. The witness list included New York's own Donald Trump as a witness for King. Trump was a casino rival to Steve Wynn and he felt he had a handshake deal with King for the rights to Douglas's next fight. He was also unhappy with John Johnson because he thought he had an oral agreement that Johnson wouldn't sign a deal with Wynn before talking to him. Johnson acknowledges such an agreement. On the stand Trump provided one of the humor highlights of the trial when Wynn's attorney mistakenly referred to him as "Mr. King." Trump responded, "I *wish* I were Don King."

Bob Arum would also testify on behalf of King. This may seem odd because the two had harsh feelings for each other that went back decades, but Arum had a fresh wound to avenge. He thought Wynn had dealt him out of the Douglas-Holyfield deal and the trial was the perfect venue for his revenge.

Don King was on the stand for three days. He was vintage, bigger-than-life King. Although he scored points in direct testimony and put on a typical Don King show, under cross-examination he had to admit to several damaging statements. King testified that Buster Douglas was a boring, lazy fighter, the kind of fighter people throw hot dogs and beer cans at. He admitted under oath that he didn't want Douglas to get up when Tyson knocked him down in the eighth round. King also admitted that he never spoke the word "rematch" in Tokyo while holding court with the press for hours while attempting to reverse the decision. Maybe Murray Kempton said it best when he described King's lawsuit against Douglas as the first attempt in the 20th century to enforce the Fugitive Slave Act.

Finally, 15 days after the trial began, Judge Sweet recessed the court proceedings and the lawyers began serious settlement talks. Johnson didn't want to settle but he would later learn that when the jurors were polled after the trial ended they basically thought there were no white hats in the room and therefore the verdict might have gone either way. Johnson remains to this day confident the jurors ultimately would not think it a just result that Douglas should be forced to accept King as his promoter considering what King admitted on cross-examination.

But Johnson would find Buster leaning towards settlement. A critical factor influencing Buster Douglas's decision to settle the case was Don King's remaining witness list. In a tactical move befitting King's tenacious nature Buster's dad, Bill Douglas, was scheduled to take the stand. Buster just didn't want to see his father go through the humiliation that would assuredly occur on cross-examination.

Steve Wynn flew into New York to confer with Johnson's attorney, Steve Enz. On July 18, Wynn and King met in Wynn's suite at the Waldorf Towers to hammer out a deal. "In the end Wynn and Enz concluded it was best to settle with King," Johnson remembered. "Considering James's concerns I went along. I have a lot of respect for Steve Enz; he is a hard working, brilliant attorney. I still consider him a friend. They asked us to agree to pay $4 million to King out of our end of the contract. I felt like we owed it to Steve Wynn so James and I agreed. But I had one condition to the deal, I told Enz that we would agree to $21 million, but Don King owed us the $100,000 and we wanted it now."

Johnson had negotiated a clause in their contract for the Tyson fight. In addition to their guaranteed purse of $1.3 million, James would receive a "bonus" of $100,000 if he defeated Tyson. King had never paid the bonus. This had really stuck in Johnson's craw.

Don King balked. The attorneys were scrambling. "You can't do this, John," one of Wynn's Los Angeles attorneys said to Johnson in the hotel suite. The two groups were in adjoining suites at the Waldorf Towers. "John, think of this as a two-fight deal. First Holyfield and then the rematch with Tyson, were talking about a $100 million total deal here. You're willing to throw it all away for a $100,000?"

Even Buster and J. D. were imploring Johnson to give it up. King requested to meet privately with Steve Wynn. After meeting with King, Wynn returned to the room, "I told King John Johnson is mad."

Johnson just turned to Steve Enz, "It's no deal unless we get the f—ing $100,000." Enz paced the room in circles looking down at the floor for several minutes. He finally looked back at Johnson. "I'm going back in there and I'm telling him you want the $100,000 or there's no agreement. But after that, I'm going home."

Johnson smiles thinking back at the moment. "I don't know what Steve said in that room but he came back and looked directly at me. 'He'll give you the money.' And the next day we got our check."

The final deal:

Douglas and Johnson would be free to fight Holyfield for Steve Wynn for a $25 million purse. King and Trump got a cut of the action, with King receiving $4 million, to be paid by Douglas out of his purse. King would agree to pay Douglas the promised $100,000 bonus for defeating Tyson in Tokyo. And King would have the opportunity to promote a Douglas-Tyson rematch after the Holyfield fight. Douglas would be free of all obligations to King, except for the Tyson rematch.

Everybody went home happy, especially John Johnson. "We did what we set out to do," Johnson said, smiling after the deal was signed. "We got James the greatest deal in sports history."

28

BETRAYAL?

It's like Coach always said, "things are never as good as they seem or as bad as they seem."

—John Johnson

If the most important thing in life for John Johnson is loyalty then what Buster Douglas did to him after Tokyo can only be described as the ultimate betrayal. But personal betrayals are complex and not always easy to analyze. Whenever two people are involved in a long or intense relationship, trying to sort out the true cause of the divorce is tricky business. Even today John Johnson bristles at the notion that Buster betrayed him. But what happened between them cannot be easily ignored.

"I just thought nothing would ever come between us," Johnson says quietly as he tries to understand what happened after Tokyo. Johnson struggles with words while sitting in the small office in his suburban Columbus, Ohio, home. "We'd been through so much together. You know you don't get to the world heavyweight championship fight without living and dying together. I guess it's like a marriage."

Johnson sheepishly smiles at his analogy. John and Sue Johnson had just celebrated their 40th wedding anniversary. "I know I'm part to blame. I let things get too far away from me. When we got back from Tokyo I was very busy negotiating the contract for Buster's next fight and setting up endorsement deals, so I decided to hire a couple of Buster's old friends from high school. I thought it would help him deal with his new life and keep us focused for the next fight. It turned out to be a mistake."

Angelo Dundee's comments in his interview with Larry
Merchant ring true here. The sport of boxing is a true team effort
both in the ring and outside of the ring, and the Buster Douglas–
John Johnson team was beginning to unravel. "It seemed to be
the perfect idea at the time," Johnson said. One of the friends
mentioned above [Johnson refuses to provide his name, stating
he doesn't want to "show him the respect" of appearing in the
book], claimed to have an accounting degree, a claim Johnson
later found out to be false. The other friend, Rodney Rogers,
Johnson hired "just to be with James." Johnson also hired his
son, Johnny, Jr., to work with the press. Johnny has a degree in
Broadcast Journalism from Ohio Wesleyan and had eight years'
experience in sportswriting.

Before the real problems began Buster and John traveled
together for goodwill work. Their travels took them to the Los
Angeles Hollywood Palladium to support Henry Belafonte who
was receiving the Nelson Mandela Freedom Award (Johnson met
Gregory Peck in L.A.—one of Johnson's greatest thrills). They
traveled to Chicago to meet Walter Payton to help raise money
for an inner-city basketball program. They went to the West Virginia Golden Gloves tournament to meet and sign autographs with
Muhammad Ali. Buster testified before Congress on behalf of
low-income families needing assistance with home heating bills.
While in Washington, D.C., Johnson and Douglas would also attend a fundraiser for the homeless. Another fundraiser for an inner-city youth center took them to Atlantic City where Buster
received the key to the city. They also did several charity events
in Columbus. The media criticized Johnson for organizing these
trips but he and Douglas both felt a deep obligation to use this
moment to help those less fortunate.

The stress was starting to show, however. Johnson was trying to line up endorsement deals, and Douglas was neglecting his
workouts and putting on weight. One morning three months after
the fight at the Mirage hotel in Las Vegas, Johnson asked Douglas—who was with his two friends—if he'd ran that morning.
Douglas said he had not, and, as Johnson put it, "Coach Hayes

was coming out of me." McCauley convinced the two to take the argument up to Douglas's suite, where Douglas promised to start running the next day. He did not, though, but disarmed Johnson at the time.

The final incident that pulled the team apart came after a Columbus high school event. Buster was invited to speak to the Marion Franklin baseball team before the state tournament. What Johnson didn't know was one of the new members of Buster's inner circle demanded a $500 appearance fee from the high school. Johnson never would have authorized such a deal. Johnny, Jr., overheard the request and, like his father, he wasn't shy about his reaction. "I guess the apple really doesn't fall far from the tree," John Johnson would remember the incident. "Johnny is a passionate and compassionate young man. He thought what they did was wrong, and so do I." An argument ensued and Johnny ended up hitting Buster's friend with a legal pad full of loose papers. No one was hurt, but the feelings were running high. Johnson called Douglas and demanded that he fire his friend. The next day, to Johnson's dismay, Buster had the young Johnson fired instead. The elder Johnson cleaned out his desk as well. "It was one of the saddest days of my life," Johnson reflects back. "In a couple of days James called me and told me I had done a wonderful job handling his career and negotiating their contracts, but from then on he was going to make his own decisions—without my advice."

Jerry Page told Johnson that it seemed like he went "from being 'the greatest guy who ever lived' to being an ass overnight," remembered Johnson. Johnson admitted, "Well, I was an ass before. I was the one who got in his face and told him 'you have to do this' and 'you can't do that' and motivated him to become heavyweight champion of the world."

You've heard this story before, new-found fame clouding sound judgment, and stubborn pride preventing partners from sitting down and talking—until it's too late. "When I finally did intervene things had gone too far. In hindsight, I guess I waited too long and when I did reassert myself it forced Buster into a corner. After that we weren't a team anymore. It makes me sick to think about what happened to our team. In the beginning and all the way to Tokyo all of us around Buster had one single goal, to do whatever it takes to help Buster get the championship belt. But after Tokyo the new people weren't really thinking of Buster's interests, it was all about them." Johnson looks visibly shaken 16 years after the fact. "I was extremely depressed. In fact, if you think about it, after a big match like Tokyo is when a fighter needs aggressive guidance more than ever, especially someone like Buster. Look, here was a guy who never had this kind of exposure and he's a shy guy to begin with. In hindsight he needed John Johnson at his best, it may have been my most important role as Buster's manager." Johnson seems to drift away for a few seconds. "I guess, in a way we were both out of our element, this was new territory for me, too." Johnson grabs for something from under his desk. It's Woody Hayes's book, *You Win With People*. "You remember this book, don't you?" Johnson asks as he thumbs through the pages. "It's like Coach always said, 'things are never as good as they seem or as bad as they seem.' Boy the Old Man loved his Emerson didn't he? How many times did he quote from Emerson's book, *Compensation*? I guess we weren't thinking of old Ralph Waldo after Tokyo. Maybe if I would've just reread Coach's book things might've turned out different."

So just how deep was the rift? "There was never a true split," Johnson explains. "I was in the ring with Buster when we fought Evander in Vegas, but we weren't the same team we were before. I had no say in preparing Buster for the Holyfield fight. Once you go down the path of avoiding a situation it's tough to turn it back around. And the longer you let it go the harder it gets." Even Steve Wynn saw it. On a trip to Vegas in his private jet before the Holyfield fight Wynn called Johnson up to the cockpit and said, "Keep your mouth shut, John, anything you say *they're* opposing you at every turn." Wynn shot a glance back at the new group that surrounded Buster in his jet. On more than one occasion, Douglas had been told Johnson said something that Johnson claims he never said. "I tried to explain to James," said Johnson, "but the look I got broke my heart and I could see he didn't listen to me anymore."

Johnson kept his mouth shut, but held out hope of still being an influence. "I was thinking that when the fight started [against Evander Holyfield] I was going to be in the corner and then they couldn't shut me up. Somehow I thought I would be able to help him win the fight. I was wrong." Johnson's encouragement wouldn't help against Evander Holyfield.

Douglas gave it everything he had, but Holyfield caught him with a great punch and it was over. "Did he prepare properly?" asks Johnson. "No." Johnson pointed to Douglas's mother's death and the controversies and distractions surrounding the fighter. "Not to make excuses . . . but I guess it was too much."

Johnson consoled Douglas in the locker room, quoting Teddy Roosevelt's famous line that it is not the critic who counts, but the man in the arena who strives valiantly. "Hold your head up high," Johnson told him, "for you have been in the arena."

He would, however, never be world champion again. We will never know, as John Johnson so fervently believed, if Buster Douglas would have been the greatest champion ever. Fame was fleeting indeed.

SEVENTEEN YEARS LATER

All a man can say about his hair going gray is that it beats the hell out of the alternative. One doesn't have to ask John Johnson to know that would be *his* response. His hairstyle hasn't left the sixties (although it's now completely gray), and he's still wearing those same Michigan gold pants around his neck. His talk and his walk are slower, and he's added a gold cross earring—an adornment not contemplated until after Woody Hayes's death in 1987. Johnson spends time with his grandchildren and his dog, Angel. He continues to believe in dreams, and to him loyalty is still the most important trait in life. Most importantly of all, he's back with Buster. "I love Buster Douglas. We made history together." The two went about 14 years without speaking after the Douglas-Holyfield fight, but are "once again friends with, I think, a mutual respect and love for each other," says Johnson.

And what about Buster Douglas? Well, the soulful, baby face is still there, and even though he's far from his top fighting condition, Buster looks like he could still go a few hard rounds. I sure as hell wouldn't want to get in the ring with him. He's never left his home or the old Blackburn gym. Buster spends his days in Columbus with his wife Bertha raising his two young sons and managing his baby brother's boxing career.

In the end Buster and Buster alone will ultimately have to live with the person in the mirror (as all of us will), the person who came to the brink of his own destiny only to have it brush past him like an illusion. For isn't it enough that a man ventures great risks and sacrifices public attention for his dreams to come true? Shouldn't a man be satisfied with the sheer simplicity of the achievement itself? Should a person suffer responsibility for

anything more than that? Or will Buster Douglas's missed opportunity to attain the greater illusive immortality haunt him forever? He was heavyweight champion of the world thanks to one
perfect afternoon in Tokyo.

BIBLIOGRAPHY

Personal Interviews

John Johnson, Buster Douglas's manager, interviewed by Bill Long

Pete Johnson, All Big Ten and All American OSU fullback and all-pro running back, interviewed by Bill Long

Jim Lampley, ESPN boxing analyst, interviewed by Bill Long

J. D. McCauley, Buster Douglas's trainer, interviewed by Bill Long and John Johnson

Larry Merchant, ESPN boxing analyst, interviewed by Bill Long

Angela Pace, Columbus, Ohio WBNS-TV 10 (CBS affiliate) anchor and community relations director, interviewed by Bill Long

Aaron Snowell, Mike Tyson's manager, interviewed by Bill Long

Joe Theismann, ESPN football analyst and former all-pro quarterback, interviewed by Bill Long

Books and Articles

Berger, Phil. "Mike Tyson: Tales From the Dark Side." *M Magazine*, January 1992.

McIlvanney, Hugh. *The Hardest Game: McIlvanney on Boxing*. Edinburgh, Scotland: Mainstream Publishing Company, 1995.

Mollet, Clinton. "Mike Tyson's childhood." EastSideBoxing.com, March 16, 2004.

Newfield, Jack. *Only in America: The Life and Crimes of Don King*. New York: William Morrow & Company, 1995.

Oates, Joyce Carol. "Mike Tyson." *Life*, March 1987.
Plummer, William. "Cus D'Amato." *People*, July 15, 1985.

THE AUTHORS

John Johnson is the former manager of James "Buster" Douglas and the president of Coach Boxing, Inc. A former graduate assistant football coach at The Ohio State University under Woody Hayes, he is still trying to win another world championship. He has coached in six world championship fights and three Rose Bowls. He lives near Columbus, Ohio, in Westerville.

Bill Long graduated from The Ohio State University in 1970 with a degree in Fine Arts. While attending OSU Mr. Long played quarterback for the legendary football coach, Woody Hayes. After attempting a career in professional sports he enrolled in law school, where he was bitten by the political bug. The bite lured him into a 25-year lobbying career. Long's first book is a novel titled, *Black Bridge.* He is presently working on two new projects, a second novel and his next non-fiction sports book. He lives in Columbus, Ohio.